From GRACE to BOTHAM

Profiles of 100 West Country cricketers

David Foot

THE REDCLIFFE PRESS
BRISTOL

First published in 1980 by
Redcliffe Press Ltd, Bristol

ISBN 0 905459 27 X

Printed in Great Britain by
Burleigh Ltd, Bristol

CONTENTS

3

CONTENTS

Illustrations

5

FOREWORD

My affection for cricket is considerable but clearly I didn't watch every one of the hundred players who feature in this book. I only imagine that I did. Some I gazed at in awe from my improvised seat on the boundary or in the press box; others were folklore heroes. I read every word about them, chuckled at the apocryphal stories and did my best to separate the documented fact from the good-natured hearsay.

I reached my century of portraits in this book and quickly realised there were reprehensible omissions. Where were Ken Palmer and Graham Atkinson, Gilbert and Langdon? I rattled joyfully away at the typewriter as players came to mind—and in the end I had to pull up stumps before the long, lovely list was completed. My hundred are not necessarily the best in terms of cold statistics; many of them, however, were distinguished cricketers who by sheer merit, strength of personality or endearing eccentricity left their mark on the history of Somerset and Gloucestershire cricket.

Only five current players have actually been included. I've also tended to look back beyond the immediate past and hopefully there will sometime be another book to incorporate the Brains and Brassingtons, Burgesses, Taylors and Dennings.

You will find a minimum of statistical detail on the following pages. Mostly the career records take account of county matches only, although other first class achievements are included in the case of some of the players. The interpretations of character and whims are my own; others with longer memories and different attitudes may just occasionally disagree.

I have looked to friends like Andy Wilson and Bill Andrews to confirm an impression or provide an elusive detail. Grahame Parker's *One Hunded Years of Gloucestershire Cricket* has been a valuable guide; so has the Lord's library and its helpful custodian Stephen Green. I have been assisted by Tony Brown at Bristol and Tom Tout at Taunton; by Michael Hill, Somerset's diligent statistician, Nico Craven, Neil Harvey and John Mace.

West Country cricket has a particularly rich—and at times, riotous—texture. I hope I've managed to stir a few happy memories and convey something of a remarkable breed: all the exhilarating way from W. G. Grace to Ian Botham.

BASIL ALLEN
(1932–51)

Basil Allen was at heart a country gentleman. After he scored his last pugnacious run for Gloucestershire, his emotional home was the rolling hills of Mendip rather than the more claustrophobic county ground in Nevil Road. He hunted with an enthusiasm which was once more directed to cricket. As Joint Master he had the bearing and reputation of a Somerset squire.

At Clifton College he had the build of a natural sportsman. His head, which should have been full of learning, was inclined to wander to sporting pursuits. Public school honour was usually at stake on a Saturday and he spent the evenings in search of extra batting practice. As a player he had a penchant for suicidal fielding and, when it was his turn to bat, to pull and sweep the ball powerfully, although his defensive play was intense. Gloucestershire sages would look across the Close and nod approvingly to themselves. It seemed the most natural thing in the world for him to do what others had done before: make the cricketing journey from Clifton to Ashley Down.

Allen, born in 1911, had his first game for Gloucestershire when he was 20. In that first season he made more than 600 runs. There were not many signs of nerves and Grahame Parker, later to be secretary-manager, will recount graphically a partnership with this zestful newcomer; it was worth 151 for the seventh wicket. Young Allen went on to make 85 off a tidy Hampshire attack. Then he moved on to Cambridge, waiting a year for his Blue, celebrated with a neat half-century.

His batting style appealed to Bristol, Gloucester and Cheltenham crowds. He struck the ball with the kind of power that comes with a sharp eye and nimble feet. Soon he was getting his 1,000 runs a season for Gloucestershire. There were memorable stands with Reg Sinfield, Billy Neale and, of course, Wally Hammond on the way. His own technique was developed

9

and strengthened by the skills he saw around him; but then business commitments limited his appearances until 1937 when he took over the captaincy after the untimely death of D. A. C. Page. The responsibility brought an added dimension to his play. Other players responded to him and the county won 15 matches. They finished fourth in the championship table. Allen himself was now looking a very useful batsman. His maiden century came against neighbouring Somerset at Taunton. There was soon another against Derbyshire and, sweetest of all no doubt, one against Yorkshire in Bristol. In 1938 Hammond and Barnett were off playing against the Australians and depleted Gloucestershire dropped down the table. But Allen still scored 1,500 runs and deservedly earned the newspaper headlines of the day by hitting 77 against Derbyshire after spending a day ill in bed.

He wasn't everyone's idea of a captain. There was at times a touch of the martinet about him and certainly in the post-war years at least one young professional experienced a few stinging reprimands from this disciplinarian. Offsetting this was his sense of justice. 'He was above all a fair man—and loyal to the younger players,' said a contemporary. He could also be an imaginative and positive skipper.

It came as a surprise to many when he stepped down in 1939. Hammond turned amateur and took over. As for Allen he played only a handful of matches that season but still possessed enough concentration to be the only player to reach 50 in a low-scoring game on a difficult wicket at Bristol against the champions, Yorkshire.

He rose to major in the Somerset Light Infantry and then loyally returned to Gloucestershire. Hammond had already gone in 1947 when Allen so nearly led the county to the championship title. It agonisingly slipped away on a maddeningly worn pitch at Cheltenham. That decisive match with Middlesex remains one of the peaks of cricketing drama within the county. Supporters died a hundred deaths and continued to ask a hundred hypothetical questions long afterwards. Basil Allen, who shared the anguish of all the other players as the county eventually lost by 68 runs, surely relived all of Cheltenham's heartache and exasperation as he regularly crossed the Mendip contours in search of the fox.

He may have lived in Somerset but his ties with Gloucestershire remained strong. For two years he was the county president, until 1980.

Record: 13,265 runs (av 29.47)

DAVID ALLEN
(1953–72)

Was there ever a cricketer with a temperament better suited for the Big Match? David Allen never winced when an insensitive soul swung a ponderous bat and undeservedly cleared the fence at mid-wicket. He stood impassively at the crease, in the much recalled Lord's Test of 1963 as Wes Hall thundered towards him, hopefully on the scent of last over success. Allen, the country's survival balancing on his square, motionless shoulders, could have been playing a third-form match at Cotham Grammar School.

At least that was the illusion. Beneath the exterior of apparent unconcern, the mental concentration was built up into an impenetrable wall. Derek Shackleton had gone and there was only Colin Cowdrey left, broken arm encased in plaster and privately recoiling from the involuntary heroics of the situation. Hall, all brawn, coordination and fearful speed, bowled the last two on a perfect length. Allen did not flinch and the match was drawn.

So, typical of the caprices of the game, my most durable memory of the Gloucestershire off-spinner is of his phlegm in the fading light of Lord's. England could not have found a better man sensibly to thrust a straight bat at the pitch of the intended lethal missile. Allen allowed himself an esoteric mutual smile with Hall and strolled—he seldom seemed to break into even a trot—back to the pavilion for a ruminative pint before motoring down to Bournemouth to join his wife.

11

He played 39 times for his country and but for the occasional lapse of logic on the part of the selectors there would have been more Test appearances. I bade him goodbye and good luck on a banana boat at Avonmouth in 1959 as he was about to leave with the England team for his first Test series, in the West Indies. It was supposedly a press conference. But R. W. V. Robbins, who had called it, was tetchy and unnecessarily protective. Peter May the skipper was taciturn and the younger players seemed wide-eyed and overawed. It took fatuous subterfuge on my part to fight my way through the Eldridge and Fyffe crates for the dastardly motive of wishing a Bristol friend well.

Allen, who possessed a nice, dry sense of humour, possibly appreciated the comic breach of security. He went on to play with great success on tour over the seven winters that brought him, with domestic international honours, 122 wickets. Usually he played better abroad than at home; interestingly he had more success, it could be argued, with his country than with Gloucestershire. Bristol's wicket had no embracing love for his well-flighted spinners. It did not help, either, that he and John Mortimore were in the same county side. Two such splendid off-spinners seemed almost like an indecent luxury.

At Gloucester, Cheltenham, Lydney and alongside the witheys at Stroud, before the bulldozers chased surly singles all over the square, I saw Allen bowling at his most challenging. There was no more than a token run-up, and economy of effort characterised the whole process. But the brain was still working intensely. Like many spinners, whatever their academic credentials, he was a cricketing intellectual. He was no computer.

Some expected him to become a Gloucestershire captain and perhaps he would have liked the job. His personality did not allow him to be an eye-catching tearaway in the field. A few, unfairly, even claimed he was indolent. He was both intelligent and sensitive.

Allen started with club cricket—and returned to it after he had finished with the county. This helpful, well-meaning trend is less common than it should be. He does not mind village blacksmiths boasting in their cups that they have clouted a Test bowler for six. He's blessed with a sense of perspective and it is revealed in the remoter rural cricket dinners, where he proves himself a willing and fluent speaker.

Record: 882 wickets (av 22.13) 7,510 runs (av 18.59)

BILL ALLEY
(1957–68)

Bill Alley, you could say, looks like an ex-prizefighter. The features are amiably battered and the handshake from those massive fists threatens to hurl you into the neutral corner. There is a killer glint in the eyes and the broad shoulders would still surely support a bruiser's colourful dressing-gown. And yes, he used to fight for a living.

Home in Sydney he played cricket by day and boxed by night. Twenty times he stepped into the ring as a welterweight and he was never beaten. Nor did he feel pain: he broke his jaw and stayed on his feet. But maybe it ruined his chances of an Australian cricket tour. Instead, after a spell bouncing the drunks in a Sydney dance-hall, he came here to play some League cricket, marry a Lancashire lass and blissfully gravitate, by way of Taunton, to chicken-farming and the happy, unlikely mix, previously demonstrated by Sammy Woods, of deep-rooted Somerset local life with an Aussie accent.

Alley should have played Test cricket—for some country or other. The England selectors, perhaps naively thinking he was a fresh-faced newcomer just down from university, actually studied the current batting averages one Sunday morning in committee and pondered his inclusion, until whispered information arrived that he was a middle-aged pugilist from the other side of the world. To complete the pedigree, the confidant could have added that Bill was one of five sons of a modest local government clerk and had earned an ertwhile crust as a black-smith's striker and a boilermaker's mate.

Somerset did well to bring him from Lancashire. No one had really heard of him in the West Country. And not too many prophesised a lengthy stay when he initially paraded a succession of unsophisticated pulls and scythe shots. In front of the Taunton tavern, prim geriatrics looked aghast. Mendip clerics nervously pulled at their dog-collars. How were they to know that William Edward Alley, a wonderfully unique and unsubtle talent, was on the point of scoring the first of his 24 centuries for the county?

He stayed with Somerset until the late sixties and continued to pull and scythe his shots outrageously. Opposing skippers populated the leg-side boundary with fielders who rubbed gentle palms on the turf in anticipation of a catch out of the clouds. Mostly he still eluded them, pitching his lofted blows infuriatingly just between them or toweringly out of their reach. On Festival grounds like Weston and Bath he had a mischievous penchant for landing his sixes first bounce on the trestle-tables in the beer tent. Wary barmen ducked for their lives and put him up his first pint of the evening.

His 1961 season was phenomenal. He scored 2,761 runs for Somerset alone and finished with more than 3,000 from all first class matches. Whenever I looked in at a Somerset match he was at the wicket. Most of the time he was chattering and cussing away, in a manner which amused or irritated according to your point of view and current bowling analysis. He wasn't remotely a stylist but how magnificently he struck the ball. He scattered spectators, spraying his shots as if he were flicking corn to his hens at home.

Team mates at times did not quite know what to make of him. He growled and occasionally blasphemed. He was often immensely good company. He enjoyed his hand of skittles as much as any Somerset lad.

Alley was nearly 40 before he played his first game of cricket for the county. He was almost 50 when he left rather abruptly, speaking his mind honestly as ever and talking of being given 'a kick in the pants'.

He wasn't simply a hitter of great gusto and skill. He was a medium-paced bowler, who could get unexpected movement and could keep batsmen quiet all afternoon. And there was nowhere a safer boxer's pair of fists at gully. When he put his pads away he predictably missed his cricket and was soon back as an

14

umpire, rising to Test match status. His decisions didn't always please everyone.

Woods also was something of a boxer. Somerset never threw open its pavilion door to two more welcome Aussies.

Record: 16, 644 runs (av 30.48) 737 wickets (av 22.07)

C. J. BARNETT
(1927–48)

Charlie Barnett liked to work up an appetite for lunch. He was never noticeably inhibited in the early overs when more circumspect batsmen were governed by the glistening dew still lying in the outfield. He liked half volleys and hunted for them.

Barnett played in 20 Tests, a dozen of them against the Australians. They didn't exactly take kindly to him at Trent Bridge in 1938. At lunch he was 99 not out. There was not too much respect in the way he carted the tourists. He scored his hundred with the first ball after the interval, with an almost apologetic shrug.

He came from a family of cricketers. Several of them played for Gloucestershire; father Charles Sherborne, an amateur with an emotional leaning to the professionals, actually captained the county. There was no lack of cricket conversation and counsel around the dinner table or in the family business. Young Charlie was thrilled with the way his father could open the innings for Gloucestershire. His own tentative chance came in 1927 as a 16-year-old.

There was plenty both right and wrong with him at first. He was strong off the front foot and his bold driving impressed county pundits. But he could also be reckless. He was inclined to be indiscriminate and had a natural antagonism to extreme caution, even when it was needed. He did well enough in 1928, however, to be given an extended run after several trial matches. Then came the offer of a professional contract. 'Take it,' said his father.

He knew where he was going wrong and worked diligently to

15

improve his defences. Blissfully he refused to abandon his care-free aggression. He would also, apparently, accept a cheeky challenge. Somerset's Bill Andrews, a great admirer of Barnett, reminds us of an occasion when Gloucestershire needed just 26 to win when they opened their second innings. Andrews claims he was on perfect length and line but the opener unconcernedly hit him for 20 in the over. Then Barnett was out to the first ball of the big Somerset man's next over.

'I had Harold Gimblett to thank for that. He'd gone up to Charlie and bet him ten shillings he wouldn't belt me over the stand. And Charlie for once picked the wrong ball!'

By 1933, Barnett was taking over as opening bat from Dipper and was looking a much more responsible and mature cricketer after the rushes of blood in the first three or four seasons. He attractively hit half a dozen centuries, reached 2,000 runs and earned a first Test appearance against the West Indians. The England recognition came at the last minute. He seldom suffered from nerves: he walked out at the Oval at No 8 and made 52 before he was run out. There followed an MCC tour of India.

His career is full of dazzling displays—and some ducks. There were centuries before lunch against Glamorgan at Bristol and Somerset at Bath in 1934. There was never a hint of slog-ging: the strokes were good to look at, the innings handsomely built. There were three Tests against the New Zealanders two years before the war—and a knock of 232 at the Wagon Works in Gloucester on a day when Lancashire were not bowling at all badly. And there was his capable, accurate seam bowling which, but for a few dropped catches and coats of varnish would have brought him 400 wickets.

Barnett was very much a Gloucestershire man and it showed in the responses of the crowd. In some ways he had the manner of the amateur; he was a good man to have around when the professionals wanted to make a point.

He was still around, although coming to the end of his Gloucestershire days, in 1948. The third day of the match with Yorkshire looked ominously like defeat for the home county, especially as the Bristol wicket was wickedly taking spin by then.

The interest locally seemed academic: Gloucestershire needed 389 to win in four and a half hours. They won with 45 minutes to spare. Barnett (141) and Emmett, impervious to the vagaries of the pitch, scored 226 runs in two hours. After that the county were home and dry.

That is the only way to remember Charlie Barnett.

Record: 21,222 runs (av 31.96) 371 wickets (av 30.36)

IAN BOTHAM
(1974–   )

So where do we start? Not with statistics, which he spectacularly changes in the time it takes to dash off a paragraph of praise about him. He mocks cautious predictions by those who say he can never keep it up; we dust off the superlatives and, in Test terms, they are almost immediately obsolete as he supersedes them with his next personal triumph.

Ian Botham was captaining England by the age of 24. In that same May of 1980 he was chasing to his first double-century with an outrageous speed and belligerence that must have been in the Jessop class. There will be more to come: as surely as he wills himself to land a wily, elusive salmon, shoot a pheasant or score goals for Scunthorpe Reserves (to the delight of South Humberside fans and the despair of cricket sages, who worry that his fitness will be impaired.) No one, he implies, need worry on that score. His chest muscles are like iron bars and he will bowl all day if necessary. He likes to dismiss the first six batsmen and then put the winning hit out of the ground. He has a sense of the dramatic to match his own considerable gifts. In a crisis he volunteers to shoulder the taut responsibility of bowling the final over.

He has been called brash, abrasive and over-confident. He has been known to offer an expressive reaction to braying spectators who do not understand what is going on at the wicket. His eyes flash readily and one or two of his more publicised 22-yard feuds, like that with New Zealand's Hadlee, have been part of the growing-up process. He doesn't suffer fools or those who try clumsily to rile him at an Australian barside. Discernibly he has matured as a person. Like Brian Close, one of his mentors—and one-time goaders—he can be refreshingly sentimental. He is tender with his family; and a good companion with a sense of fun.

Botham's parents are from Yorkshire and they, both of them, played cricket. He was brought up in Yeovil but the North Country approach, all granite and adrenalin, is always there. At school he preferred soccer to rugby and nearly joined Crystal Palace. Instead he went to Lord's for his apprenticeship, sorted out the art of swing bowling and clean striking of the ball, and made his debut for Somerset when he was still 18. Within two years he had his cap, within three a place in the Test team.

Since then he has made cricket history with a tingling precocity. He scored 1,000 Test runs and took 100 wickets faster than anyone else. The game's historians will cite other records; there are doubtless more to come. Whatever that makes him, he is certainly neither a run-machine nor the best fast-medium bowler to walk out with the England players at Sydney or the Oval. Arguably he is the most enthusiastic and the one most likely to turn Wisden into an autobiography.

An aggressive, unloving bowler, he can at times swing the ball away from the right-hander as well as anyone in the current game. He is also quite capable of moving it the other way. His yorker is much feared; so is the bouncer, occasionally devalued by him through over-use. A flaw in his multi-sided personality is apt to show when a batsman starts inconsiderately hooking him to the fence. Exchanged glares are legendary and lethal.

At the crease, Botham can be stirringly entertaining. On his purposeful walk from the pavilion he swings his bat several times through an arc of 360 degrees. It looks as lightweight in his hand as a golf club. He has a good deal of style, as well as sheer power. The off-side drives are sweet and assured and he can swing the ball hard and high to square leg, down on right knee and already smiling triumphantly to himself, with savage skill.

He must be involved in every facet of the match. His fielding, either close to the wicket—where he tends to offer constant advice—or in the deep is sharp, brave and reliable. When he fails, as he did with the bat at times in Australia in the 1979–80 series or at times for Somerset, he feels it personally and his demeanour spells out his frustration. Mostly he does not fail.

LEN BRAUND
(1899–1920)

Whatever possessed Surrey to let Len Braund pack his bags and leave? They watched him in practice, youthfully affecting guile with his leg-spinners and, with a folly they were soon to regret, they decided he was precocious rather than promising. So Len, who had a more realistic appreciation of his own ability, calculated that if native regard for him was so scant he might as well move. He came to Somerset—and went on to play 23 times for his country.

No doubt he privately harboured the less than complimentary assessment of his all-round talents by erstwhile Surrey committee men. Team mates sensed an additional resolve in his play against the county which once gave him no more than the occasional match. If Surrey made him impatient, so did the game's bureaucrats. They made it difficult for him when he first arrived in Somerset and delayed his registration while he became residentially qualified. That arch opportunist, W. G. Grace saw no reason to keep a good man out of action: he invited Len to play plenty of cricket for him at the Crystal Palace.

Braund was born in 1876. From earliest schooldays it was his ambition to play for Surrey. Whether that county's apparent indifference to him was political or indicated an appalling lack of perception we shall never really know. Somerset were far more intuitive. In the 1899 season he played five innings against the Australians and scored his maiden century against them at the Crystal Palace for a delighted Dr Grace. His first appearance for Somerset was also against the tourists. He scored 82 and reminded them he was not a bad bowler, either.

From 1901 he was seldom out of the Somerset side unless needed for the Tests. He goes into the record books with other great county all-rounders like Sammy Woods, Arthur Wellard and Ian Botham. At his best, Braund was a devastating slow right-arm bowler in the finger-spin tradition. Three times, like Wellard, he achieved the double. In addition there was his catching at slip. If Hammond was the safest and most efficient slip fielder in the West Country, Braund was a close second. He took 508 catches for Somerset, many of them made to look ludicrously easy.

The pattern of selection in Somerset was also, he discovered, inclined to be bizarre at times but at least there was never a question of his omission. His first summer for his new county brought him three centuries and more than 1,000 runs, as well as 79 beguiling wickets. Reports from the relatively unfashionable West Country needed no pigeon to prod the MCC selectors. If he could spin his way through the defences of Plum Warner and 'Ranji' for The Players at Lord's, he had to go that winter to Australia.

Braund was 25 when he made his first tour. It was not a great series but Braund's contribution was singularly impressive. He scored a half-century and took seven wickets when Australia lost the first Sydney Test by an innings. Going in at No 7 at Adelaide, he was 103 not out at the end. In all the tour matches, he scored 737 runs and took 118 wickets.

Home again he virtually beat Yorkshire on his own at Sheffield. His spinners were angling wickedly and he finished with 15 wickets. Then after some indeterminate form with bat and ball he re-asserted himself with 141 against The Gentlemen.

He had a cussed streak, as well as a companionable nature, and success in that particular fixture always pleased him. When he travelled off with Warner's party to Australia again in 1903–04 he made a century at Sydney and took nine wickets at Melbourne.

For a time the runs became more elusive; worse, the magical fingers began to let him down. No longer could he persuade the ball to make its disconcerting detours. Length went as well. Suddenly he realised he had lost the cricketer's noble art of spin.

He gave it up, puzzled and probably annoyed, and got on with his batting. In 1913 he hit a magnificent 257 not out in less than four hours at Worcester.

Braund reappeared briefly after the war and then retired. In the years that followed he often returned to the county ground for a happy reflective chat and drink. He died just before Christmas in 1955. In any context he was one of the great Somerset players.

Record: runs 17,801 (av 25.61) 25 centuries wickets 1,113 (av 27.30) Catches: 508

BERTIE BUSE
(1929–53)

In his very earliest matches for Somerset, when he popped over from the solicitor's office in Bath to send down a few deceptively innocuous overs and prod runs of punctilious patience, the county records rather impersonally registered him as 'Herbert T. Buse'. Those of us who went on to snooze uncomplainingly through his innings and exchange knowing looks at his under-rated talents as a seam bowler knew him, even if a boundary-length away, as Bertie.

He was that rarity among cricketers: he could make un-entertaining play hugely entertaining. His batting was stodgy, unimaginative, one-paced; and yet a Taunton or Bath crowd never became restive. There was affable banter around the tea-tent but hardly ever a hint of reprimand. The reasons are not hard to find. One was the nature of the man. He was modest and amiable. In conflict with the style of his batting, he allowed himself many a grin. His manner was prim and John Arlott likened him to a butler bringing in the tea. But he was an immensely engaging butler who we imagined might permit himself the isolated indiscretion below stairs at least once a year. There was self-parody in Bertie Buse, the Cricketer, and it was an endearing quality.

Somerset can seldom have had a more phlegmatic player. He

21

hid his emotions until you looked, close-up, into those twinking eyes. Worcestershire came to Taunton in 1951 and needed five to win off the last ball of the match. Bob Wyatt unconcernedly hit a straight six into the pavilion. The bowler, Buse, allowed himself a wry smile. Theoretically, he was the one Somerset man who would never have allowed such a liberty. His bowling was unwaveringly tight, marginally short of a length and difficult to punish.

Bowlers usually all came alike to Hammond. He could be slightly grudging in his praise for the medium-pace genre but more than once he generously singled out Buse. Bradman was less respectful, although that is another story altogether.

Even in the immediate post-war years a uniformity was beginning to appear in county cricket. There were fewer faded caps around from the major public schools and academic by-ways. Players were looking more alike, aping each other's styles and mannerisms. Buse, from the City of Bath School, remained very much identifiable. The bowling run-up was wholly his own. He started with a perfunctory walk as though he was taking a Sunday afternoon stroll along Great Pulteney Street. Then he offered a little medieval jig, hops of delicate, balletic balance, followed by a sudden, disconcerting acceleration. There still wasn't too much impetus by the time he reached the wickets but the ball was hurled down with the kind of thrust that revealed reserves of strength in those shoulder muscles. The length was unerring; he seamed the ball with his head as well as his fingers.

As a batsman, too, there was no mistaking him. He crouched in ungainly comfort, all 'bat and bum'. His broad bat did not let too much go by, though the moment of contact was not the most exhilarating of experiences on a cricket field. As for his bottom, it sprawled itself with the conservative contentment of a Rhode Island hen basking in the evening sunlight an hour before roosting-time. Wicket keepers prayed for better vision.

We detected hints of the robot in his batting. But the centuries came along and were warmly cheered. Just occasionally he would parade a thrilling square and late-cut before touching his cap apologetically and receding once more. Somerset, let it be remembered, usually had a surfeit of batsmen who were raw, reckless and ravenous for runs. Buse, whatever the deficiencies of his stroke-play, could give the innings sanity.

He was a valued all-rounder in the tradition of Ernie Robson. As a bowler he could produce genuine movement and had a late in-swinger to trouble the most proficient of batsmen. With Bill Andrews' help, he bowled out the Indians before lunch in 1946 (5–27) and I did not miss a single vigorous shine of the ball on his trousers in what was the most marvellous pre-lunch cricket of my life.

Bertie belonged very much to Bath, where once he was a fine rugby full-back and a table tennis champion. There was financial disaster in his 'one-day' benefit in 1953 but his lengthy association with Somerset, going back to stray appearances as an amateur in 1929, brought mutual reward.

Record: 10,623 runs (av 22.65) 657 wickets (28.77)

SAM COOK
(1946–64)

Sam Cook was an uncomplicated man. As a plumber home in Tetbury, he did not turn the bathroom piping system into a veritable Clapham Junction. He was a reliable, old fashioned craftsman and he brought those same unlittered skills to his slow left-arm bowling. He turned his arm over all afternoon, the honest journeyman, hopefully hunting out the chink in the batsman's defence as if he were methodically trying to detect an irksome leak in the attic plumbing.

There was no plumbing but plenty of cricket for him during his Air Force days in Rhodesia. A Worcestershire man recommended him to Gloucestershire and he turned up, unknown and uncertain about the county ground protocol, for the pre-season nets. He had a nice homely walk, the kind that belongs to a small country town pavement on the carefree amble between matey pubs on a Saturday lunch-time. He recognised Wally Hammond, coughed and said: 'I'm Cook'. A pause as the Master eyed him, searching for more explanation. 'Cook—from Tetbury'.

Cook from Tetbury was encouraged to get into some flannels and show the assembled company what he could do. He went straightway into the 1946 side and took 113 wickets. His very first ball, straight and measured, maybe going just marginally with the arm, earned him an Oxford University victim. Gloucestershire simply had to give him his cap before the summer was over. He kept taking 100 wickets nearly every season until 1958. There was no especial wizardry about the way he tossed the ball up. Accuracy was more evident than imagination, good nature more than bowling malevolence. The so-called golden sands of Bristol, sarcastically likened to the expansive beach of Weston-super-Mare by a score of disgruntled opponents from Jack Meyer to Brian Close, were very much to Cook's liking.

'With Cookie at one end and big Tom Goddard at the other, what chance did a batsman have at Bristol just after the war unless he had a bucket and spade with him?' cynics used to ask. This was where he finished with 9–42 against Yardley's Yorkshire in 1947. They were the best figures of Cook's 18 years with Gloucestershire, although not necessarily his best bowling. The pitch was a faithful ally and the temperature was furnace-high in the Yorkshire dressing rooms.

Like rather too many under-valued West Country cricketers, Cook made a solitary Test appearance. The creases in his flannels were immaculate for the Trent Bridge fixture with the South Africans but he knew it was no pitch for him. His nine overs cost nearly 90 runs and he wished fervently he was back at Tetbury. As some compensation he was No 9 in the batting order.

His batting was, in fact renowned for the limitations of his shots. Some generously said there were two in the repertoire. Cook himself sniffed at such disparagement. He once hit a resolute 35 not out, appropriately in his benefit match, and walked to the crease with a discernible Cotswolds swagger on the days Gloucestershire shot him up the order—to No 10. He scored more runs than he took wickets: but there wasn't so much between them.

At times he headed the national bowling averages and finished the 1962 season on that lofty perch. The accolade did not noticeably affect his pleasantly one-paced way of life. Statistically, 1956 was his peak. He bowled away all day when asked to, found the greatest difficulty in being inaccurate and ended with 149 wickets. That was the year he had Kent comically reeling at Cheltenham as he took 7–11. At Stroud three summers later I watched him gently spin his way to 5–13 against Warwickshire, who could make absolutely nothing of him. I can still see his happy, bronzed, perspiring face as he came in to the applause. He looks equally content with the world now, as an umpire.

A Gloucestershire countryman at heart. Give him a cricket ball in one hand and a pint in the other (with maybe a couple of plumber's spanners in his pocket) and he was at peace with the world.

Record: 1,768 wickets (av 20.26)

C. C. DACRE
(1928–36)

Gloucestershire did well to get Charlie Dacre in the first place. He had come over with the New Zealand tourists and had every intention of swinging his bat merrily and then going home again. At Cheltenham his aggression seemed to impress everyone. That was in 1927 and those with long memories claim he scored his first 50 in a quarter of an hour. Over a drink later he was being asked by refreshingly opportunist county committeemen: 'Feel like staying, old boy?'

Dacre liked the idea, even more when some timely research persuaded him that he had family ties with Gloucestershire. He continued flailing his bat to score more than 1,500 runs for New Zealand, including four centuries. By this time other counties were understandably beginning to sniff. But his hosts at Cheltenham had been first. He decided to qualify and by 1930 was sending Worcestershire fielders off on countless vain chases to the ropes. In his most devastating innings for his new county he scored 223 that day to disrupt the ecclesiastical calm of

Worcester. Over the next five years he reached a century 15 more times. Dacre was always worth seeing at the wicket. He was strong on footwork, crisp of shot. He could adapt if suddenly the innings had to be held together; but he was happiest when he could dictate. There are warm memories of fluent and fiery partnerships with Hammond. Dacre frequently opened the innings and at Worcester in 1933—he clearly liked that ground —he and Charlie Barnett were at their most ruthlessly exciting. They put on 196 before lunch for the first wicket. Dacre scored a century in each innings; so, for the record, did Hammond.

Five times he reached a century against hapless Worcestershire who had neither the bowlers nor the heart to curb him. Gloucester and Cheltenham both saw him at his best in 1934; four of his centuries were reserved for Bristol where his popularity at times equalled that of the great Hammond.

Dacre in full flow was one of the joys of the thirties. He hit the ball with great power and seemed equally at home with the fast and slow bowlers. There was for Gloucestershire the bonus of his flawless fielding in the deep, and an ability to keep wicket with real efficiency. The great disappointment came in 1936. He appeared to lose something of his self-confidence and zest and it was not a complete surprise when he parted company with Gloucestershire. In a comparatively short time he had an exciting influence on the county of his adoption.

Record: 8,271 runs (av 28.32)

JOHN DANIELL
(1898–1927)

John Daniell frightened the life out of some of the young professionals. He had an intimidating manner and an assertive way with words, making him an autocratic captain and an authoritative secretary of Somerset later. He was called 'The Lion of Judah'—out of earshot. Certainly he belonged to the old school and did not take kindly to pros with a mind of their own. When Bill Andrews once found himself in the role of dressing-room militant, intrepidly suggesting the terms of a revised contract, he claims that Daniell—by then club president—bit through his pipe in rage.

No one should under estimate his influence on Somerset. The county needed a tough and single-minded administrator, if not a genius, to hold them together in the haphazard years before and immediately after the First War. He was captain—on his own terms. He invited his chums to play, and went sniffing around the universities in search of potential talent.

Daniell was an astute judge of a rugby player but occasionally wayward when it came to cricketers. There was a non-existent vetting system and a long line of amateurs, fresh-faced with romantic youth or rubicund from perhaps excessive claret, made their Somerset debuts. They took precedence over the disgruntled professionals in the batting order; mercifully some did not stay for long. A few drove the skipper to distraction with their eccentricities. Robertson-Glasgow, one well worth his place, favoured fielding in a staw hat. When he lost his travelling bag and took the field in his black walking shoes. Daniell wouldn't let him open the bowling. 'What are you doing in bloody dancing pumps?' he thundered.

Born in 1878, Daniell started making runs at Clifton College. He won his Blue at Cambridge in 1899 but by then had already played for Somerset. When he was 30 he took over from Sammy Woods as captain for the first of his two spells. He reckoned that a skipper should be in the side very much on merit; as such he was heading the batting averages very soon and hitting an impressive century against Lancashire at Bristol. His batting could be accomplished and watchful although he would suddenly emerge with venomous swings and sweeps, usually being caught at long-leg in the process. It was fun while it lasted and earned him popularity with the crowd. The bowling strength was invariably uncertain in the years that he led the team, from 1908–12 and 1919–26. Generally he handled his bowlers well and set a fine example in the field. Some of his best catches were taken at silly point. He deplored shoddy fielding and he had to contend with plenty. There was a puzzling turnover of players, especially in the vacations, and specialist fielders were a luxury.

Ask any Somerset diehard to nominate Daniell's finest match. It was the one with Essex at Taunton in 1925. The captain scored 174 in the first innings and 108 in the second. He hardly gave a chance, even though he was hobbling badly by the end of the game because of a knee injury which kept him out of cricket for some time.

He had his last matches for Somerset in 1927 before turning to the administrative side of cricket. Some believed his affection for rugby was even greater. He had played for Cambridge and captained England three times against Ireland and three times against Scotland. He was a selector for England at both rugby and cricket.

According to son Nigel, himself a former assistant secretary of Somerset, John was 'probably the greatest judge of a rugby player there has ever been'. He was also a cunning bird when it came to outwitting the press. Nigel tells of the time a reporter arrived at the England team's hotel to interview the captain W. W. Wakefield. To shield the player on the eve of a big game with Wales, Daniell successfully impersonated 'Wakers'. That reveals he was an actor, too—and one with the impressive physique of a rugby star.

Record: 9,824 runs (av 21.78)

GEORGE DENNETT
(1903–26)

Some cricketers, it has always seemed to me, win less retrospective recognition than they deserve. Maybe they suffered because their style was not theatrical enough. The slow bowlers usually earned fewer headlines than the fiery hitters. They were the game's general labourers and as such didn't spawn nostalgic anecdote in the same way.

George Dennett was a classic case. He must have been a marvellous bowler for Gloucestershire, trundling away with gentle cunning and undeviating precision for over after over. As a left-arm slow bowler he was not quite in the class of the man who succeeded him in that role, Charlie Parker. But did Parker's rare skills cause us to be reprehensibly forgetful of his predecessor?

Dennett, a quiet, likeable man, had been enjoying his weekend cricket around the clubs in Bristol when Gilbert Jessop brought him into the 1903 side. He stayed until 1926 and in that time took more than 2,000 wickets for the county. Indeed only Parker and Goddard took more. He did it with a minimum of tricks; he could spin the ball but not disconcertingly. At times, on a capricious wicket, however, he could be virtually unplayable.

It is not difficult to pinpoint his greatest game. In every sense 1907 was a wonderful summer for him. He began by going to Gloucester where the Northamptonshire batsmen's morale must surely have been destroyed for the season. They were all out for 12 in the first innings. Dennett virtually won the game on his own—he followed up 8–9 with 7–12 including the hat-trick. That was one of the occasions when the slow bowler stirred the wing-collared scribes to extol his self-effacing virtues. He went on to take 201 wickets, the first time that a Gloucestershire bowler had topped 200.

Like so many talented players raw to the game, his first season had been a modest one. He may have bamboozled his friends at The Clanage or even Sleepy Hollow but county cricket was shatteringly different. Bright-capped amateurs, down on vocation with ideas of fleeting drama, swung at slow men like young Dennett with cross-batted irreverence. He was left surveying horrendous bowling figures and pledging privately a hasty return to club conviviality (and more success). Jessop and others had their doubts about whether he could survive these early experiences. They sensibly persevered; and he rewarded their faith by heading the bowling averages the following season.

He had some sort of distinction in causing Parker reluctantly to keep going with his seamers for a long time; there was really no room for two similar bowlers. The pair frequently opened the attack and, of course, there were long periods when the county relied almost entirely on spinners. Few sides were more bereft of genuine pace.

At Bristol in 1906 Dennett superbly went through the Essex

innings on his own. In 1913 he did the hat-trick at The Oval, a rare achievement by any standards. That day he took 9–63. He once took 16 wickets in a match against Hampshire at Bristol and his consistency is reflected in the fact that from 1904 up to the outbreak of war it was unthinkable that he would end up with fewer than 100 wickets a season. He averaged nearer 150.

He was given a benefit in the match with Kent at Clifton College in 1920 and was still accurate enough to take 107 wickets the next season. When he retired in 1926 he was appointed coach at Cheltenham College. Between the showers he was occasionally persuaded by the boys to tell about the rout of Northants in 1907 and, what probably gave him more native pleasure, the day he had Somerset going with an eight wicket spell on an unresponsive wicket. Friends claimed he was equally proud of his one innings of 71.

Record: 2,082 wickets (av 19.88)

A. E. DIPPER
(1908–32)

Alfred Ernest Dipper was a poker-faced countryman who occasionally allowed a smile to flicker across his lips. It did during the first innings against Glamorgan at Cheltenham in 1923. Miraculously a solitary ball found an almost imperceptible chink in the batsman's redoubtable defence. It trickled wickedly on to the stumps—but the bails stayed on. And Alf went on to make an undefeated 252. He scored 22 not out in the second innings and was on the field for the whole of the match.

That is one of the famous stories about Dipper. The re-telling is embroidered with innuendos, never malicious, about his ungainly build. He was hardly the most agile of the Gloucestershire players. He was not sharp in the field nor, especially, between the wickets. But his stirring stamina at Cheltenham in the early twenties was clearly a revelation.

Dipper was rural in features. His stance at the wicket was splendidly unsophisticated and if he sensed that opposing players gave each other sideways looks it scarcely bothered him. He had monumental concentration, argued faultlessly that the primary job of a No 1 batsman was to stay at the crease and made no obvious concessions to cheap popularity. Nothing flustered him. He would shuffle his feet between deliveries and tug more determinedly on his cap when opposition crowds tended to bait him. He was not the game's best conversationalist but reckoned that his batting figures had their own undynamic eloquence. Between 1908–32 he scored 53 centuries for Gloucestershire. He played just once for England against the Australians. That appearance, to open the innings at Lord's, brought great private joy to this basically unemotional man. He made a typical sound, unspectacular 40 in the second innings but was never chosen again.

'It was your fielding, Alf,' they used to say to him later. 'That was what let you down.'

He would contemplate the statement for a long time, then say with a justifiable sting in the retort: 'I had 197 catches for Gloucester'. And so he did, many of them well taken in those knarled agricultural hands of his. He seldom put the ball down when it came straight at him.

Dipper was a right-hand bat of solidarity rather than style. He had no great flexibility and had his own reliable, if restricted, range of shots. Most of his runs came on the leg side. He was quite capable of hitting the ball heftily past mid-on, not often in the air. Risks and wristy flourishes were anathema to him. He got on with the job at his own pace.

That pace is at times remembered a trifle disparagingly. Dipper was an invaluable batsman to his county. For a long time he carried the innings. When the young Hammond arrived the rushes of blood perplexed Dipper. He unconsciously improved Hammond's defence by example. The debt to Alf was occasionally acknowledged in later bar-room conversations.

Dipper's first innings for Gloucestershire were at an undistinguished No 9. It took him three seasons to establish himself and score 1,000 runs. After the war he carried on as before. There was a century in each innings against Sussex, a knock—galloping by his standards—of 247 against Oxford before a poor crowd at Bristol and 2,000 runs a summer for much of the twenties. Opponents groaned when he loped to the wicket. And so they should have: he carried his bat 11 times, more than any other Gloucestershire player.

He fancied his bowling like many opening bats. He was modest slow-medium with the ability to bowl a few cutters on the right wicket. In the years after the war he came on at about second change and was good enough to take 52 wickets, for instance, in 1919.

Record: 28,075 runs (av 35.22) 161 wickets (av 30.32)

GUY EARLE
(1922–31)

Guy Fife Earle had a roguish disregard for the niceties of self-promotion. There was seemingly neither tact nor required courtesy in the unsubtle way he heaved the ball through the window of Taunton's Dickensian press box. Somerset's staid scribes of the day sensed the pending danger and comically took cover from the splintered glass under those sturdy and distinctive ledger-desks. It was no way to treat your publicists; but Earle, maybe with more strength than sensitivity in such matters, was already plotting the direction of his next six as the cluster of wan reporters emerged unscathed to pursue the pretty prose and sedentary decorum once more. Journalistic trench warfare was something to be savoured in retrospect.

Earle quickened the pulse and intensified the warm glow of schoolboyish expectancy as only the greatest and most prodigious of the county's hitters could. Arguably he was less refined in the extrovert art than the others. His technique had the flaws which, back in his Harrow days, drove cricket coaches to distraction. He joyfully predetermined his smites and was inclined to execute them with wanton cross-bat vigour. Seldom, for instance, did he hit straight and true in the manner of a Wellard or Tremlett. The short Taunton boundary turned cricket at times into a plaything for him. At Weston-super-Mare's

The scoreboard tells it all: Somerset's great first wicket record stand between Lionel Palairet and Herbert Hewett against Yorkshire at Taunton in August 1892.

Guy Earle—the smiter; Bill Andrews—the (young) enthusiast; Harold Gimblett—the Master; Bertie Buse—the 'butler'.

Clarence Park he impishly flicked honest, middle-stump balls away to leg over the conifers.

He belonged undeviatingly to the amateur genre and had just a few of the less personable traits that went with it. But mostly he was an approachable and popular figure: and so he should have been with that mischievously reckless philosophy traditionally beloved by the Somerset pundits.

Earle was born at Newcastle-on-Tyne in 1891, with a background of modest privilege and sporting instincts. He went to Harrow and ended up captaining the school at cricket. He became part of Harrovian folklore. He was just coming up to his 19th birthday when he led them in perhaps the most famous and recounted match with Eton. Harrow should have walked it; an extraordinarily noisy crowd of 10,000 at Lord's were convinced they would. The statistics weighed heavily against Eton who were forced to follow-on 165 runs behind. A sluggish pitch did not help and Eton were a paltry four runs ahead with one second-innings wicket left. Inspired aggression by unknown batting talents after that caused Harrow to go in again needing 55. And they lost by nine runs. A young man called Fowler, not content to have been top score for Eton in both innings, went on with his uncomplicated off-breaks to take 8–23. The disbelieving Earle was later criticised on two counts—for keeping himself on to bowl too long and then opting for the heavy roller.

Maybe this revealed a slightly too dogmatic side to his nature. Team mates were apt to say later that his tactical judgment was suspect. They never faulted him, however, for the excitement he generated and his indifference to opponents' reputations. He toured Australia and New Zealand in 1929–30 with Harold Gilligan and in the fixture with South Australia he squared up to Grimmett, taking a perfunctory 22 off one over. Three of the shots were venomous sixes.

Earle had a brief flirtation with Surrey but qualified by residence for Somerset in 1923. He was soon showing the West Country what he could do. The size of the Bristol boundary momentarily disconcerted him after the cosiness of Taunton; then he slashed his way to 111 in just under an hour and a half.

His outrageous fame was quickly established. The day he smashed the window in the press box, his share of a 58-run partnership was 54—in 35 minutes. His dismissal often seemed imminent; but his eye was ruthlessly sharp. In the time it takes to walk from the Crown and Sceptre to the ground in Taunton, a quarter of an hour, Earle scored 59 against Gloucestershire.

His nine seasons with Somerset were punctuated by such surrealistic swings. He toured India with the MCC in 1926–27, once gobbled up 130 runs on an otherwise somnolent day at Bombay and cherished an electrifying stand with Maurice Tate which confused the scorers by adding 154 in just over the hour. His final tour was to Egypt with H. M. Martineau's party in 1932. He was hurt in a motor cycle accident and forced to retire prematurely from the game.

It seemed worthwhile at last to mend the press-box window. Record: 4,627 runs (av 18.96) 87 wickets (av 28.14)

GEORGE EMMETT
(1936–59)

George Emmett was the son of a soldier. The military man's neatness of appearance, precision of manner and sense of discipline were instilled in him. A few of the younger pros occasionally found it slightly tiresome. They still liked him—and envied the rich texture of his batting.

He hit 34 centuries for Gloucestershire, most of them in a controlled hurry. The wrists wrote poetry. He was a small man and we should have been more conscious of the stretch as he leant for the half-volley. There were plenty of these, effortlessly created by the instinctive movement of the feet. Yet for all the perfect balance and the delicate stroke-play he was never fully fit after returning to the county from his ack-ack regiment.

Emmett hobbled out of the war with a painful knee. Arthritis set in painfully and it was noticeable in his running between the wickets or when he turned swiftly in the field. Stiff joints were not a valid excuse, alas, and Wally Hammond dropped him twice in the first season back, in 1946, when the crowds bulged animatedly and hungrily over the boundary and Emmett scratched uneasily for runs. Gradually the gentle stylist's touch was restored. He would steal away for his knee treatment before the match and hope that he could disguise the disability. Runs—and that often meant boundaries—were the best healer or at least, anaesthetizer of all. He could be prolific on the leg side but his cover drives had the positive zest of a Hammond. He learned much from the Master.

When Hammond had gone and Graveney was still on the way, Emmett was the side's experienced artist. There was nothing untidy or ragged about one of his innings. He was looking for shots much of the time and at times 'nibbled' impatiently. He could be strangely nervous and was out nearly 30 times in the nineties. Afterwards, in his role as tutor, he advised assertively against all the little human errors that he made himself.

By 1947 Emmett, prim and pocket-sized, was readjusting to the physical demands of the county game. He carried his bat against Oxford University and scored a century in both innings at Leicester, something he imperiously achieved again in the match with Somerset at Bristol four years later. In 1949, 1951 and 1953 he topped 2,000 runs. Those summers were liberally sprinkled with hundreds and the kind of shots that were talked about long after, in the bar.

The Test selectors were cussedly myopic when it came to West Country virtues. They looked only once to Emmett, to the surprise of many of his admiring contemporaries. He did tour India, his birthplace, twice with Commonwealth teams. Ironically he had nearly joined Somerset in 1935; Messrs White & Co were perhaps embarrassed at the prospect of yet another left-arm spinner. That, in fact, was part of his appeal when he turned up at the Bristol nets with his flannels a year later. He promptly took 48 wickets in his first season. After that, he was left to get on with his batting. In retrospect, his recession as a cheeky spinner is to be regretted. Some said, with pardonable exaggeration, he could turn the ball at right angles.

Which was Emmett's best knock? His highest was the

memorable 188 against Kent at Bristol in 1950. Three years later he impishly squirted his way to a second innings century when Lindwall and his formidable Australian chums came to Bristol.

Everyone, however, seems to nominate the flawless 127 off the Lancashire bowlers at Bristol in the August of 1958. That was Emmett at his most brilliantly mercurial. He was the smallest player on the field and yet he dwarfed everyone with a maestro's performance. As he walked in at the end, dapper and upright despite the limp, crowd and players rose to him.

Record: 22,806 runs (av 31.45)

HAROLD GIMBLETT
(1935–54)

Ah yes, Harold Gimblett: my hero, and the hero of every Somerset boy who sniffed Taunton's freshly-cut grass in early April and already envisaged this impetuous genius at the wicket in the first over of the day, casually lofting fours as if he were tossing hay, home at Bicknoller.

His cricket embodied panache and pleasure and ultimately pain. There were tortuous psychological battles never far away. He suffered the manic depression of another much-loved Somerset player, Roberton-Glasgow. He was one of the county's greatest batsmen but the self-doubts and complexities of his mind would not allow him to sit back and enjoy the rare, natural gifts he brought to the game. At last, in the Spring of 1978, the time of year when emotionally he was closest to the sport he both revered and incomprehensibly reviled, he took his life at the age of 63. We mourned him and many friends walked the few paces from the county ground to St James's Church, in their shirt sleeves, for the memorial service. As the address began, we could hear the applause for a Richards six. It seemed wholly appropriate and not mildly disrespectful.

Gimblett hitch-hiked to the small Frome ground in the May of 1935, went in at No 8 and scored a century in 63 minutes. It was his first county match and was straight out of schoolboy fantasy. He hated talking about it, squirming every time it was romantically re-quoted on the sports pages and at club dinners. The farmer's son was more photographed than royalty for those few artificial days after the Frome debut. He never managed to cope easily with publicity.

No player was more self-deprecating. He decided he could not hook or shape right for in-swing. He was 'hopelessly inadequate' in dealing with leg-spinners. Or so he said. His record proved differently, When he was in full flow, they all came alike to him. Early on, however, despite his fearlessly swinging bat at West Buckland School, he had a patently vulnerable defence. Secretary John Daniell gave it to him straight after a month at the nets. 'You're no bloody good!' Gimblett reflected later: 'I was furious. But he was probably right'.

Daniell, seemingly a wiser judge of a rugby player than a cricketer, suggested that Gimblett was a better bowler and fielder than batsman. That was an ill-advised assessment. The player, just turned 20, set about tightening his defence and before long was opening the innings. He still went on swishing, like the run-happy Watchet lad he basically was, at the ball rearing away, outside the off stump. He still gave up his wicket to an astute opposing skipper prepared patiently to buy it after dropping his fielders back on the ropes.

Gimblett magnetically lured cricket-lovers and excitement-seekers to the ground whenever there was a chance he was batting. He could stroke the ball quite beautifully, always with fiery persuasion rather than brute force. He was a master of timing, a model batsmen for all the aspiring young cricketers in their school caps, who chased to the ground after the final period of the afternoon. There were 50 centuries from his eloquent and saucy bat. His highest innings was 310 against Sussex at Eastbourne in 1948. I heard it on the six o'clock radio news and nearly choked, I remember, on my home-made raspberry jam. I remember it equally well for the way I went straight out in the garden with my modestly-hewn bat, tried a Gimblett cover drive and put the tennis ball through the front-room window.

The war years robbed him, like so many, of thousands of runs.

He still zestfully picked up the traces with seven centuries in 1946 including 231 against Middlesex at Taunton. His best season was 1952 (2,134 runs). Others scored more in a season, none apart from Viv Richards so instinctively. His thick forearms belonged to farming stock and there was strength as well as timing in his hitting. The stance, like the appearance, was neat.

England's selectors were criminally cautious and beckoned him only four times. The last, a belated summons to savage the spin of Ramadhin and Valentine, never materialised because of an untimely and much-headlined carbuncle. After a relative failure in his first Test, Gimblett despondently changed and started walking unseeingly round the ground. A kind man demonstrated with his umbrella where Harold was going wrong. It was Jack Hobbs, and the young pupil went out and made 64 in the second innings.

Record: 23,007 runs (av 36.17) 41 wickets (av 51.80)

TOM GODDARD
(1922–52)

Tom Goddard appealed for LBW more than anyone else of his day. The shout was loud, bass-like and with the dogmatic authority of a man who presupposes he will never be turned down. It is said that umpires, new to the list, seldom failed to concur. Some of their more experienced colleagues were slightly less charitable.

Gloucestershire's magnificent off-spinner hardly ever hit the batsman's pads without shouting. There was not an iota of gamesmanship in his spontaneous call for dismissal. It was unthinkable to him that a batsman who played him and missed was *not* out. Goddard played his cricket with an uncomplicated passion. He was not necessarily always the best judge of when the ball was capable of hitting the stumps.

He was a towering man with a natural bounce in his deliveries, quite apart from a marked facility to spin the ball. If it was hazardous when umpiring to him it was even worse as a wicket keeper. Normally the bowler used a short third man and not a slip. That was the stumper's preserve, quite apart from the acute difficulties of keeping track of a wickedly turning ball, momentarily lost as it crossed the batsman's body.

Goddard, like that great goalkeeper killed in the Munich crash, Frank Swift, was said to have hands like buckets. His fingers entwined themselves around the seam and the spin could be prodigious. Those lovely big Gloucester artisan hands were also made for catching. As he followed through, he appeared to narrow the angle for the batsman, making mid-on and mid-off superfluous. He took many a sharp return catch, mainly one-handed. There was no bravura in the process: catching simply came casually to him. But it was then good to see his face light up. A catch off his own bowling was a schoolboy fantasy relived.

He was born in 1900 and came to the county as a fast-medium bowler when he was 22. Successes were meagre and Goddard, slightly lugubrious by nature, looked like losing heart. He went off to Lord's—and came back an off spinner. The transformation astonished everyone; he immediately took more than 150 wickets.

His Test debut followed in 1930. Goddard went on to play in eight Tests. It was criminally scant reward. The pundits still looked quizzically at off-spinners and the selectors refused to be impressed by the Gloucestershire man's mountainous list of victims. In 1937 he took 16 wickets against Worcestershire at Cheltenham. He did it again at Bristol two years later and pulverised the formidible Kent batting side by taking 17–106 at Cheltenham the same summer.

Those 17 wickets were gobbled up in a single day. By doing that he equalled a world record previously shared by Colin Blyth and Hedley Verity. Records as such did not make too much impression on Tom. He possibly said: 'It would have been 20 if those shouts hadn't been turned down'.

It could be argued that one or two of the home wickets were very much to his liking. He could do magical things with the ball at times in Bristol. He was more of an illusionist at Cheltenham where batsmen were apt to spar at what seemed like a mythical ball.There was an ageless determination about him. In 1947 he was taking 238 wickets and he was past 50 when he finally gave up.

Goddard, in the jargon of today, needed no motivation. He was very much a competitor and professional. He waged a personal battle with every succeeding batsman—as the fingers effortlessly twitched, the ball hummed through the air, high and challenging. Off the field he was relaxed and happy with a pint in his hand, warmly ready to talk of the wife he adored, an afternoon's fishing or . . . the plum LB that for some unknown reason was turned down.

Record: 2,862 wickets (av 19.58)

E. M. AND G. F. GRACE
(1870–96) (1870–80)

There were five of those brothers, born at Downend and trained by mother in an orchard at the back. Indoors there were as many cricket books and prints as medical publications. County status was the natural progression, by way of Rodway Hill, Thornbury, Stokes Croft and a score of undulating meadows where wary Shorthorns populated the outfield.

E.M. was the third son and Fred the fifth. Neither threatened to emulate W.G.'s prowess although in their different ways, of style and temperament, they were richly talented. In a melancholy moment of brotherly contemplation, The Champion said through his tears at Fred's premature funeral: 'He would have been the best of us all'.

G.F. was just 30 when he died of pneumonia. All the medical knowledge in the family couldn't save him. A fortnight earlier he had made his first and sole Test appearance. He had a duck in each innings; for someone so full of life and promise, he deserved a better memorial than that. The Test had been the first ever played in this country between England and the Australians. W.G. was the captain and was the only one of the three Grace brothers playing to make any impact. He treated the Oval crowd to a gritty innings of 152, steered England to a win by five wickets and tactfully spoke up for E. M. and G.F. over a drink to pre-empt and snide references to nepotism.

Fred, in fact, was worth his place on his fielding alone. He was dashing and elegant in the outfield, expert at judging the towering catch and sprinting 50 yards to save a boundary. From the moment he was eagerly introduced to serious, competitive cricket at Canterbury in the late sixties, he practised with an engaging enthusiasm, rather than unrelenting dedication to be a successful allrounder. He had ten years with Gloucester-shire, from the county's first days, and picked up nearly 170 wickets. All four of his centuries were made on the Close at Clifton. The controlled aggression was good to watch. In 1873 he scored 165 against Yorkshire and two years later reached 180 against Surrey. Neither time was he out—nor did he look like being out. The Champion looked on proudly. Fred was his favourite brother.

E.M. had a sterner face and a more intractable approach to cricket and life. Everyone called him 'The Coroner', based on the legal duties which took up his time in North Gloucestershire, between games, if not innings. Coroners do not smile. They determine the cause of death and express sympathy to the relatives. One could imagine E.M. cataloguing the grisly details in laborious longhand. His innings were compiled in the same intense, rather doleful way.

Edward Miles Grace must have been, all the same, a fine all-rounder. When he was invited to tour Australia, it was matter of merit and not solely brotherly influence.

The Graces were never really more than a wicket's length away from controversy. It started for E.M. when as a 21-year-old he was rushed, relatively speaking, from Downend to Canterbury to play in two matches. The first was for Kent and all was well; the second, as a slightly surreptitious condition of the journey from the West Country, was for an MCC XI against Kent. He certainly had no obvious qualifications to join the MCC team and the dressing-room dialogue was noisily contentious for a long time until the Kent players, for the sake of a game at least, relented.

41

Young Grace, backed up by his father who was on holiday in the area, showed no benevolence to the county side. He could not understand what all the fuss was about. As the simmering disapproval continued, he summoned up all the concentration that a few of the bowlers seemed to be lacking. He scored a brilliant 192 not out—and cheekily took all ten Kent wickets in the second innings. Kent's rancour was understandable up to a point. E.M. had been out first ball when playing for them.

There were some monumental innings from him in club cricket—as a hundred battered but lovingly preserved scorebooks still testify. He scored just three centuries for Gloucestershire but he was an integral part of an emergent county. He was the first secretary and stayed in office till 1909, two years before his death. He refused to have too much nonsense from dissenting committee members and once let it be known how displeased he was when W.G. was given a benefit before him.

Records:

E. M. Grace 7,859 runs (av 18.11) 171 wickets (av 23.50)

G. F. Grace 3,279 runs (av 28.26) 166 wickets (av 19.24)

W. G. GRACE
(1870–99)

He has been dead since 1915 and his awesome, vastly bearded presence still dominates the county headquarters, even if he did stride away from Nevil Road in a huff. He was The Champion; that truly meant the best of them all. No batsman let fewer balls pass him. The runs multiplied to staggering proportions. So did the stories, half of them authentic, about his unique skills, his gamesmanship and his sulks.

W.G. was a national figure as famous as Gladstone. He and his family launched Gloucestershire cricket. The Grace brothers spectacularly took the county to the top of the table four times. Faded record books remind us that he was human enough to fail just occasionally. Mostly he was phenomenally successful. He first walked out as a slender and callow 15-year-old at No 9 to

42

score 32 against a formidable All England XI on the Downs in
Bristol in 1863. And he simply went on from there.

With inexhaustible energy, unbelievably accommodating
attitudes from his medical locums and a single-minded devotion
to the game, he played at every opportunity. He knew obscure
train timetables almost as well as the personal bank balance he so
diligently surveyed. In 44 years of active cricket he scored nearly
55,000 runs and took almost 3,000 wickets with his 'devilish
difficult dolly drops'. There were 126 centuries. The 100th of
those is probably the most comprehensively documented. It was
against Somerset in 1895. Sammy Woods led the applause and
reckoned that only five balls got past the bat. One of those, he
good-naturedly contended, had the Old Man LBW. There were
plenty of shooters on some of those rough-and-ready wickets of
the day. W.G., more effectively than any of his contemporaries,
developed a technique to counter the sneakiest of daisy-cutters:
he trailed his bat uncommonly low to the ground as he played
forward.

He enjoyed being a celebrity. There was no affected false
modesty and the post-match adulation was happily accepted in
that distinctive high pitched voice of his. The compliments were
heavy and well-wined at the celebration dinner to mark his '100
hundreds' at Bristol's Victoria Rooms. He got to his feet, none
too reluctantly, to respond to the tributes. His stamina was as
remarkable in the social as the cricketing sense. That evening he
drank as liberally as anyone present, walked out of the ban-
queting suite cold sober and immediately organised a whist
school till three in the morning.

We all know of his reputation for being supposedly arrogant,
dogmatic, cunning, selfish, high-handed and mean. He was all of
these things in part. He could also be exceptionally kind to the
professionals who laboured for him. His avarice, over col-
lections and testimonials, was the subject of bitterness and envy.
But his practice as a doctor was mostly working class and that
meant tending the poverty-stricken. He chose often to visit the
sick without thought of payment.

Some who have attempted to analyse this complex and
paradoxical man have likened him to Robin Hood. It sounds

like a glib, sentimentalised comparison. Yet it has some substance. He manipulated his expenses and organised an astonishing financial return from the game—at the expense of the game's monied gentry, the aristocrats who invited him to take part in their tours and special matches. Against that he travelled hundreds of miles at great inconvenience to take part in the benefit matches of professionals from unfashionable sides.

He was as inordinately proud of his batting as his beard. The shots were predominantly orthodox and punched away with a magical mixture of coordinated muscle, timing and supreme self confidence. Twice in 1876, at Canterbury for the MCC and at Cheltenham for his county, he passed 300 runs in an innings. He did it again in Bristol 20 years later; ten times he scored more than 200. His psychological potency was that he never remotely looked like being dismissed. Towards the end he was creaky in the bones and flabby at the waist. But he was no more ungainly than a 17-stone Warwick Armstrong captaining the Australians. He had his final game when he was 65—and still scored 69 (not out, of course).

As captain of Gloucestershire and then England he was the most eminent and revered sportsman, arguably, of his generation. His career was stacked with mighty innings, gargantuan in substance and duration and maybe less so in style. Who shall say which was the finest? The very first century, which soared almost nonchalantly to 224 not out, was the marvellous work of an 18-year-old playing for England at the Oval and must take some beating.

Gloucestershire showed him less gratitude than he deserved. Committeemen became increasingly weary of his whims, autocratic approach and self-interest. Amid mounting acrimony and after various threats, he walked out on the club in 1899. He went off to manage and lead the new London county club at the Crystal Palace instead. In a fiery finale he wrote: 'I have the greatest affection for the county of my birth but for the committee as a body, the greatest contempt'.

Time healed the schism and cordiality with Bristol—or more accurately the county committee, well represented from North Gloucestershire—returned. We prefer to remember that great cricketer, poised at the crease with toe characteristically raised, as a genial and kindly soul. The sauce of his gamesmanship and the cool way this 'amateur' made nearly £14,000 from his cricket are now relegated to jocular after-dinner speeches.

Record: 54,210 runs including 126 centuries (av 39.45)
2,802 wickets (av 18.14)

TOM GRAVENEY
(1948–60)

Tom Graveney had a batting average of more than 43 when in 1960 he chose, just as W. G. Grace had done before him, to make an abrupt and seemingly unloving departure from Gloucestershire. The parting was in fact painful and much of it embarrassingly public. He was called stubbornly peevish; if that criticism was even partially valid, the people who stuffily handled the county's administration at that time were naive, psychologically inept and blinkered.

The supposedly delicate negotiations, during which he was deposed of the captaincy were bungled at one meeting after another. There may have been a case for pondering some of Graveney's qualities as a skipper and a few of the professionals were not conspicuously enthusiastic in their backing. But he came up against the remnants of old style cricketing amateurism at its condescending worst. Old-fogey intractability increasingly taxed the patience of Graveney. He took on a cricketing free-masonry and rightly refused to sign letters that had been drafted for him. Conciliatory golf matches and cosy lunches were arranged. The great batsman, Glorious Graveney to every headline writer who had a love for the game as well as alliteration, hardened in attitude. His resignation was accepted.

The reasons why he left have become clichés. Tom Pugh, a likeable young man and fledgeling county cricketer, was unwisely appointed captain. It was humiliating to Graveney, even if he said that he would have played under Pugh or Charlie Barnett who might apparently have been dragged out of retirement to end the whole, tawdry impasse. Some at this distance continue to accuse Graveney of disloyalty and ingratitude: taunts that he ran off after pocketing his benefit were, in fact, particularly hurtful to him. Gloucestershire need never have lost him. In the end he would not compromise but he had every right to expect a fairer hearing. He had been with the county for 12 years. In that time he had scored virtually 20,000 runs for them and hit 50 centuries. He was above all a stylist. The backlift, the crispness of the shot, the follow-through made up a consummate elegance. There was always time to spare in making the stroke. He was—and still is—a splendid golfer but there was no obvious conflict of technique in the swing.

Brother Ken, later to be the county chairman, recommended Tom to Gloucestershire. They had been born in Northumberland, gravitated to Bristol and played alongside each other for the Grammar School XI. Tom then went off into the army, rose to captain rank and pondered his career when he came out. He decided he might either be a golf pro or an accountant. Ken directed him to the county ground instead.

His progress was impressive. He was a natural sportsman, whatever some of his friends said about his fielding at times early on. At school he had been a useful rugby player; he was an asset to any hockey side and he went on to become a one-handicap golfer. But it was his cricket that everyone at Bristol, Gloucester and Cheltenham came to admire. In his first season with Gloucestershire, 1948, he scored his maiden century and narrowly missed 1,000 runs despite some disappointments. The effortless cover boundaries, executed with perfect balance, multiplied and everyone seemed to be saying that the Hammond vacuum was about to be filled. After three years of county cricket he went in first wicket down for England on the tour of India, Pakistan and Ceylon. The Test Match tally mounted to 48—and the eulogistic adjectives grew in grandeur accordingly.

Some great cricketers, whatever their natural ability, will always look ungainly. The tall, slim Graveney had the appearance of sophistication. It showed in his comfortable, upright stance and the polished way he disdainfully stretched to smooth a shot

46

through the covers as if he were immaculately flicking ash from a holder.

Five times he topped 200 runs in an innings for Gloucestershire and four times passed 2,000 runs in a season for them. He was out of first class cricket altogether for one summer when the MCC penalised him for changing counties. Then he became an integral part of the Worcestershire side, helping them to the championship twice and then being elected captain, an ironic twist. They say he did not handle his bowlers well in Bristol; but there appear to have been few aggrieved pros around at Worcester. Graveney, it might be added, quietly fancied his own leg-breaks. They were unpredictable and of varied quality—but tantalising enough to bring him 5–28 in 1953. A few erstwhile Derbyshire batsmen still wryly wash down the memory of it with a drink.

Record: 19,705 runs (av 43.02)

W. R. HAMMOND
(1920–46)

Wally Hammond turned up in his bright Cirencester Grammar School scarf at Bristol Rovers and told them he was a right winger. And so he was, the fastest and best built they had ever seen in those bleak, hollow-cheeked days. He did not quite make the first team but everyone said he had that extra element of class—not just on the field. Ignoring the constraints of a £2 weekly wage as a young reserve, he moved into salubrious and pricey Clifton digs, drove up for training in a banger and paid the wife of one of the staff five shillings to wash his kit.

They also understood he could handle a cricket bat. But golf, with its plus fours and hints of social status, was always creeping into the pro's conversation. Hammond assured them he could drive a golf ball out of the ground and onto the nearby gasworks bridge. They laughed at his arrogance and he promptly and effortlessly thumped the ball high out of the Eastville Stadium. It landed in the lap of a workman sitting down to his bread and

47

cheese in a wooden hut far beyond the goalposts and the imagined Rovers' fairway.

He was more gregarious in those days. He joked as he came in first after a training circuit of the pitch. And he took out the prettier girls from the Princes Theatre in Bristol, driving them back from Weston in time for the evening show. There was still a private and self-contained streak to him; he did not confide all the time to the other young professionals, and some of them thought him deep. They put it down to the fact that he came from the outer reaches of Cotswold country, although in truth his birthplace was Dover.

The personality changed markedly, all the same, in the post-Rovers years as he established himself first as our greatest cricket allrounder and then as amateur captain of Gloucester-shire and England. He became more insular and remote. He proved himself a complex and wary man, tardy to make easy conversation and to warm to others. Team mates admired him tremendously and only feared that by some ghastly aberration they would run him out. They sensed that he was growing progres-sively away from them socially. As a skipper, his field-placing was irreproachable and his rapport with them non-existent.

Hammond was a truly great cricketer. He played 85 times for his country and scored 167 centuries in all. His cover-drive was perhaps the best there has ever been. It scorched the ground all the way to the boundary, too fast and too expertly directed for the fielders who crowded the off-side. His front-foot play was exquisite, although he could lean back and smooth the ball with equal polish and classical balance, to the fence. He was less enamoured of the pull and hook—maybe not favoured by his games master at Cirencester—but he developed and refined an effective sweep that brought him countless fours.

At the crease he had the killer instinct of Bradman. They varied in that Hammond worked by flesh and blood, as well as the kind of prototype computer programming that made bowlers superfluous. He once scored 365 not out in a boarders' match at school, presumably a jaunty run for every day of the year. By 1932 in Auckland he was scoring an undefeated 336 in the second Test against the New Zealanders. Twice in the

Viv Richards—'best in the world'; Len Braund—a great allrounder; Jack Meyer—endearingly eccentric; Brian Close—brought Yorkshire steel.

*Horace Hazell—such accuracy; Ian Botham—such swing; Maurice Tremlett
—such straight driving; Bill Alley—such belligerence.*

thirties he passed 300 in an innings against hapless Glamorgan, and once against Nottinghamshire. Four times he scored a double century at the expense of the vaunted Australian attack. The West Indies, India and New Zealand again suffered the same way. So much for statistics. Wisden and the record books are rightly monopolised by his illustrious name.

And there was not just his batting. He was a medium-paced bowler, faster off the pitch than he looked and good enough to open the attack. In 1928, off his modest run, he did remarkable things with movement through the air to take 9–23 against Worcestershire at Cheltenham. Many of his wickets came after marathon spells at the crease. He had a fine body and his stamina was never in doubt.

He was arguably the most complete cricketer of all times. As if not content to dominate the game with bat and ball, he crouched almost casually at first slip and no one ever saw him put down a catch. There was never a safer slip fielder. The catches came with ridiculous ease to him, because of his lightning reflexes and the powers of anticipation. Spectators did not see him throwing himself about to scoop catches off his bootlaces. He had the uncanny knack of pre-judging the arc of the ball and going unfussily to meet it. His partnership with Charlie Parker was almost legendary.

Hammond was charismatic and Gloucestershire supporters, who called him The Prince, rushed miles to the county ground when they heard he was at the crease. He retired at the age of 43 and we can conveniently forget the nominal appearance for a sad, solitary match in 1951. Gloucestershire's most perfect batsman and our greatest allrounder died in South Africa in 1965. Record: 50,551 (av 56.10) 732 wickets and 818 catches

HORACE HAZELL
(1929–52)

Somerset have not been too good, traditionally, at determining the value of a new contract. They let Arthur Wellard slip away prematurely at the end and it was the same, even more reprehensibly, with Horace Hazell. There were no excuses if the committee's judgment was clouded by the slow bowler's expansive middle-age waist. He always had it, and it seldom affected the competent way he picked up catches at slip or in the gully, or the saucy way he scudded for a single late in the day (and innings).

By the time Somerset were bidding him goodbye he had taken over 900 wickets for them. Only White, Wellard, Langford and Robson have taken more. He was still as accurate as ever, even if a trifle less penetrative and guileful. And he was still, in the partisan view of Somerset supporters, the best No 11 in the business. Here was the definitive roly-poly cricketer. His deportment contrasted with the dapper, snakehip vigour and movement of the eager-beavers straight from school onto the ground staff. He looked like one of those farmers who came across the road on market-day in Taunton to savour a few fours from Gimblett. He always looked happy. He bandied playful words with the spectators and relished their kindly teasing.

Hazell didn't trouble his head with thoughts of records. But his name went into the book after one incredible stint of left-arm spin bowling at Taunton in 1949. For over after over, he tantalisingly tossed up his slow, precisely-pitched deliveries. The opponents were Gloucestershire and the batsmen at the crease included the richly promising young Tom Graveney. For 17 consecutive overs and three balls (105 deliveries) he did not concede a run. One of the fielders, Les Angell told me later: 'There was a surprising amount of tension—we were all desperately anxious not to be the ones guilty of breaking this wonderful sequence.'

When he joined Somerset first, after extraordinary success as a bowler in Bristol club cricket, he had to wait with patience and increasing frustration for his chance. Jack White was the slow left-arm specialist, after all, and no newcomer is precocious enough to think he is going to take over from an England captain. Hazell watched the crafty old 'Farmer' at work on the cricketing field, learning from him the additional value of flight and being able to nag away and pitch on that same blade of grass. Hazell never had any worries with his length, in any case, and he was not temporarily vulnerable when the batsmen, in exasperation, began to swing and audaciously use their feet to him.

He was the perfect foil to the fast men, Wellard and Andrews. There were few more economical bowlers around immediately before and after the war. Between 1946–49 he took 337 wickets and topped the averages each season. Success came to him and he met it with a sort of self-effacing charm. After a drink he liked to remind team mates that clubs such as Brislington had valued his batting, too.

Just occasionally he was elevated from the ignominy of last man. But did any county cricketer do more to raise the status of the No 11? No established batsman on 99 had anything to fear when Hazell came in to join him. The dead-bat was impeccably correct, although he liked to unleash a cover boundary of classical style and then look shyly back at Gimblett and the others gazing out from the players' window above the changing rooms.

He was often a joker. He would accept a sharp catch in the slips and pocket the ball before the batsmen looked round. He reckoned he earned his couple of bottles of Bass at lunch-time and pointed out to slightly more abstemious colleagues that he once went out and took eight wickets on the trot at Bristol after 40 minutes of such medicinal relaxation.

Record: 957 wickets (av 23.97)

H. T. HEWETT
(1884–93)

Herbert Tremenheere Hewett was the name. He was born at Norton Manor near Taunton in 1864, liked to be in charge and in his own idiosyncratic way assertively led Somerset to some notable wins in the early days of their first-class status. His tongue was apt to be gruff and he liked people to agree with him. He harboured rebuffs and had a temperamental streak that went with a strong personality.

51

Hewett was a fine left-hander and some claimed he was the best in the country. If he had been born a little later, Test recognition might have come to him. As it was, he went to America with Lord Hawke's team in 1891 and to South Africa on another tour four years later. He liked to open the innings and worked on the theory that there were plenty of loose balls around before the bowlers found their length.

He was an Old Harrovian who progressed to legal studies. Then after qualifying as a barrister he got on with the cricket for a few years. Those were tentative, experimental days for Somerset. They were not taken too seriously at first and there was a reluctance to accept them to the game's 'inner circle'.

Hewett's approach was one of no nonsense. He had a competitive instinct and backed it up with his own bold batting at the top of the order. 'The Colonel', as they sometimes used to call him, didn't believe in cluttering his innings with too much orthodoxy. He had shots all his own and his run-making had a practical, belligerent edge to it. He could hit the ball very hard indeed and hooked with the irresistible zest of the left-hander. His highest and best innings was against Yorkshire in that excellent 1892 season. It was record-making captain's stuff. He and the more introspective and correct Palairet chased to 346 for the first wicket. Systematically they tamed the vaunted North Country attack and enjoyed themselves as much as the demonstrative Taunton crowd.

As captain in the early 1890s, Herbie Hewett had the kind of tactical sense that made few benign concessions to the opposition. In the field he picked his teeth and plotted the batsmen's downfall. Over port he was said to be very good company and he would argue the virtues of the previous win with the analytical perception of the lawyer he was. When he handed over the captaincy to Woods he was not reputedly in the best of humour about one or two facets of the county club. He felt, for instance, he should have been given greater support and loyalty over that extraordinary incident when the Australian tourists came to Taunton for the first time.

The town was covered by ominous black clouds and the pitch was saturated when the umpires, in consultation with Hewett and the Australians, decided to abandon play for the day. It was a fixture which had stirred the sporting imagination of the West Country. Some spectators had walked 50 miles to be at the match and when they heard what had happened they reacted angrily. The streets outside the ground buzzed with collective disgust. But the tourists, ready for a day's break, were not complaining. They loaded a wagon with crates of ale and, no doubt, lovingly donated wortleberry pie and set off for a relaxing picnic on the Quantocks. Meanwhile the abject disappointment of the spectators, many of whom had taken a day off work for the occasion, had its effect on the umpires. They listened to the pleas of some committeemen and maybe, in any case, feared to walk out of the ground themselves. The clouds lifted marginally. As if a sop to sinking hearts, the wicket dried with uncommon haste and it was agreed that a start could be made sometime during the afternoon. Anxious messengers were sent out to find the lounging picnickers. The Australians wiped the beer froth from their whiskers and, perhaps confused by the whole thing, returned to the ground. So, after hours of verbal huffing and puffing in the pavilion, the game was played. Hewett felt he had been slighted and it rankled with him long afterwards.

He was, as his record shows, an influential member of early Somerset and would have to be considered very much on merit for inclusion as a pugnacious left-hander in any all-time county eleven.

Record: 2,592 runs (av 30.86)

GILBERT JESSOP
(1894–1914)

Gilbert Jessop favoured a heavy bat, a faded light blue cap and a crouching, almost comical, stance that was very much his own. Above all he favoured the beefy boundaries that usually defied logic. No one before or since, at his level of the game, struck so many shots so quickly in so many directions. He saw neither mischief nor madness in his joyous approach. Despairing captains sent helpless and confused fielders on endless sorties into the deep. Jessop's blows, democratically sprayed in all directions, mostly eluded them.

He did not take too kindly to being called 'The Croucher'. Nor, reasonably enough, did he relish being described as a slogger. He was never that. There was a magnificent, cussed science about his batting. The eye was sharp, the muscles taut and the feet instinctively nimble. Most of his shots, whether for Gloucestershire, The Gentlemen or England—for whom his statistics were less dramatic—came off the middle of the bat.

Jessop was not a tall man. But his shoulders were thick and there was immense strength in every movement. County colleagues envied the beauty of his co-ordination and, of course, his natural sense of adventure. He hunted for half-volleys and would fearlessly chase out to meet his bowler. The footwork was particularly exquisite: that was what enabled him to parade that spectrum of fearsome drives and cuts that encompassed 360 degrees. He could be a vicious hooker of the ball. If bowlers threw up their hands in anguish, as if to concede the psychological battle, who could fail to sympathise with them?

He played in 18 Tests and scored one century for his country. Hearts fluttered when he was at the wicket. The arrogance of his audacity, even when playing for England, had to make him something of a risk. He was not notoriously adept at changing his style and investing himself with added application because the opposition happened to be Australian. His disregard for reputation, however, was surely a large part of his appeal. Sixes in his day were relatively rare because they had to be heaved out of the ground completely but a great bowler like Rhodes was left pondering the ludicrously effortless way Jessop had scattered the schoolboys in the adjoining soccer pitch during the 1900 Yorkshire match.

Jessop came from a medical family in Cheltenham and after going to the local grammar school he did some teaching himself before going on to captain Cambridge. Grace, shrewd as ever, liked the look of him and he had his first game for Gloucestershire as a 20-year-old. His bowling was supposedly unimpressive and his fielding nervous. In fact, as a fast bowler he once took all 10 wickets when playing in East Anglia, hitting the stumps every time; and he became one of the finest cover fielders of his day.

That slightly tentative first game for his county was in 1894. From 1900–1912 he was Gloucestershire's captain. He scored 53 first class centuries and that does not include one against the West Indians. Four times he hit a century in each innings. Once, in 1903, he scored 200 against Sussex in two hours. That was the occasion he finished with his top score of 286 out of 335. His only Test hundred, at the Oval, came in an hour and a quarter. Sussex, in particular, must have been sick of him: he once opened against them at Bristol and was out in just under half an hour after scoring all 66 runs.

His scoring rate belonged more to surrealism. It averaged 80 runs an hour over an extraordinary career that was mostly alien to the purist traits of the cricket manual. He flung his bat with controlled ferocity, you could say. The uninhibited policy brought him 157 in an hour against the West Indians, 191 out of 235 in 90 minutes for The Gentlemen in 1907, a century in 40 minutes against Yorkshire at Gloucester. We could cite a score of such feats and would still be chided by county loyalists for omissions. The Jessop pattern is plain. Marvellously, rather than recklessly, he was always in a hurry.

When such delightfully indecent haste merged with impetuosity there had to be failures. He made bad shots and skied catches as he contemptuously tried to change his mind three times with the ball still in flight. There was not too much self-reprimand on his face; he was by then planning his bowling stint, and once against Lancashire at Old Trafford he took 8–54.

'The Croucher' had his final games for Gloucestershire in 1914. He was later invalided out of the army and was never in sturdy health again. For a time he was secretary of a golf club in London. He went to live with his clergyman son in Dorset where he died in 1955.

Record: 18,936 runs (av 32.53) 620 wickets (av 22.34)

55

BEVERLEY LYON
(1921–47)

Here was a captain: inventive, experimental, outrageous. He was perhaps the best Gloucestershire ever had. His calculated risks were taken with the perfunctory air of an umpire dropping coins in his pocket between deliveries. The conventions of the game never noticeably troubled him: with the jaunty challenge of the actor and the polemist he looked forward, one suspects, to the consequences.

Beverley Hamilton Lyon did it all with a fair amount of charm. If apple carts were very definitely upset as he changed out of his flannels, all was forgiven by the morning. Usually he had the players on his side, if not cricket's establishment. They whistled in disbelief at some of his tactical outrages—but preferably out of earshot. He would not have got away with it in the modern game. Professional inflexibility would have exposed and stifled his originality of thought. Above all, Bev Lyon wanted to make a game of it. He wore his trilby at a rakish angle and his whole manner suggested cricket was too rigidly conformist. He was prepared to stick to the rules—just—but was ever looking hopefully for some good-natured connivance from an opposing captain. Such co-operation was not always forthcoming. But he found it in 1931 at Sheffield.

Two days had been lost through rain and there seemed nothing much left to play for. The points system of the day was hardly an incentive for some of the last day manipulations we have become more used to in recent years. Lyon was notoriously restless in the rain. Over drinks he put a proposition to the Yorkshire skipper F. E. Greenwood. He must have been at his most persuasive. To the surprise and confusion of the smallish crowd who came along to yawn on the third day, both sides declared after scoring four byes. They were now playing for 15 points—and Gloucestershire won. They scored 171 and Yorkshire 124.

Retired clerics and peppery old military men fell in unison out of their leather chairs as news of the unpardonable ruse reached the London clubs. Letters hurtled into *The Times* with demon-bowler venom. Who was this infernal chap, Lyon? And what the devil was Greenwood doing in giving his consent? The Gloucestershire captain's ears burned and he unconcernedly took the train back to Bristol, wondering whether 15 points would placate the diehards in his old club. Some of them, forced to fidget in the temporary embarrassment of the public debate that followed, never did forgive him. His name had already been whispered as a candidate for the England captaincy. Not any longer.

In fact, Bev Lyon's only real sin was his impatience with dullness. His obsessive efforts to make a moribund game into a contest of some meaning were occasionally naive and more than once miscalculated. He had more imagination, still, than most of his contemporary skippers put together. There was a daring side to him and Freudian students might find some obscure explanation in the fact that he had two ducks in the 1922 Varsity match, when he played for Oxford against his brother, Somerset's Malcolm.

He bowled a bit of fairly gentle pace and was an agile fielder at slip or near to the wicket elsewhere. His batting was his forte; the shots were wristy and clean. By 1926 he was playing quite regularly for Gloucestershire, by 1928 he was scoring an attractive maiden century at the Oval—partnering Hammond in a stand of nearly 300 for the sixth wicket—and by 1929 he was in charge. There were in all 15 centuries from him for the county. The best was 189 against Surrey at Cheltenham in 1934 and the last was against Somerset in Bristol two years before the war.

His name still generates a conversation on its own. Elderly members who professed to know him nominate 1930 as his finest season. He would probably agree with that although he was not noticeably narcissistic. That was the summer when he scored five centuries, including one in each innings against Essex at Bristol. The memory would have been sweeter for him because he took his county to second in the championship, at the shoulder of Lancashire.

Record: 9,550 runs (av 25.39) 50 wickets (av 44.36)

M. D. LYON
(1920–38)

Shortly before going up to Cambridge in 1920 Malcolm Lyon was given a game by Somerset. He had a useful public school batting pedigree behind him and was said to play his shots stylishly. To county supporters, immune to eccentric selection and weary of seeing one young amateur after another make his fleeting, undistinguished appearance in the eleven, Lyon's name on the teamsheet brought no more than a shrug of the shoulders.

His debut was against Worcestershire at Taunton. Lyon was 22 and, like most of the others, not conspicuously troubled by nerves. But he was different from the others. He made a century. It was an intelligently constructed innings, rich in handsome strokes. The sceptics approved and the young man from Rugby School stayed in the side. He made just over 600 runs, averaged nearly 30 and was surprised to find himself top of the batting averages. There were memorable highlights in the cricketing career that followed. He made 12 centuries in all for Somerset and one for The Gentlemen at Lord's. But he played less and less during the late twenties and by 1931 had moved on to legal promotion abroad. It is pointless to speculate how much more value he might have been to Somerset.

Certainly in 1923 and 1924 he was in dazzling form for the county. He was then scoring his 1,000 runs in a season, batting beautifully against Derbyshire at Bath and excelling for The Gentlemen. At Burton-on-Trent, the Derbyshire bowlers for the second summer in succession seemed completely innocuous against him. He scored 219 in great style and the Test selectors summoned him to Trent Bridge for the trial. He made 32 in the first innings, failed in the second and was not asked again.

There had been earlier disappointments. Fresh from Taunton glory—and with the collective praise of the pundits still ringing in his ears—he won his Blue at Cambridge, and little else. He struggled for 9 in his first year and didn't even get a bat in the second.

If undergraduate cricket was unrewarding, there were better

days ahead with Somerset. He demonstrated that he was a very capable wicket keeper, quite apart from his batting. These were the happy times for him, although he realistically knew he must start thinking of his career outside the game. He particularly wanted to play against the Australians in 1926 and it turned out to be one of his finest innings. The tourists won in the end but Lyon's 136 was the ecstatic peak for the large Taunton crowd.

After that his cricket tailed away. His eye, though, was seemingly none the less hungry for runs. He played just three matches in 1928 and, perhaps with the minimum of nets, went to Chelmsford and delightfully scored 141 off the Essex bowlers. He continued, with his sporadic though significant contributions, to come out top of the averages and there were many overtures for him to play more often. In 1930 he had his final great innings. It was against brother Bev's Gloucestershire at Taunton and no runs were sweeter. They still talk about Lyon's immaculate 210 half a century later.

Record: 6,231 runs (av 31.00) 139 victims (108 ct, 31 st)

R. J. O. MEYER
(1936–49)

Somerset's cricket has been staggeringly distilled, more than that of any other county, from sheer surrealism. In more than a century, dotty amateurs of indeterminate talent and dubious geographical qualifications have breezed in to swing a virgin cross-bat and offer cricketing wisdom at the level of prep-school prattle. Some bagged a pair, dropped a dolly and made an abrupt departure for ever. A few, like Sammy Woods, were not just wondrously colourful but exceptionally adept with bat and ball. R. J. O. (Jack) Meyer stands indelibly alongside the county's eccentrically élite.

His was a sadly wasted and under-used talent as far as Somerset were concerned. At times he was inaccessible, going off to India when he could easily have been stamping his extraordinary personality on our domestic game and maybe winning

Test recognition. After the war he briefly captained Somerset; by then the lumbago was playing him up and he battled bravely for fitness.

In his days at Cambridge he rightly fancied himself as an opening bowler. He had a nice, controlled action and was already developing the knack of swinging the ball late from leg. His bat could be both exciting and ill-disciplined. He had a surprising array of natural strokes and by the mid-thirties, back from India and now teaching in Somerset, there was added responsibility in his batting.

R. J. O. was a man bored by blind insistence on the orthodox. He was one of cricket's philosophers and whetted his appetite with daring, at times imprudent, experiment. As a bowler he simply wouldn't stick to medium-paced swing. He'd suddenly throw a leg-spinner into the permutation. He was quite capable of bowling six different balls in an over. It could be bewildering for the batsman, and even worse for Wally Luckes behind the wickets. He had a good-natured autocratic attitude to the game. He was not the best of time-keepers, according to some of his contemporary professionals. The more cynical pros exchanged winks or gestures of resignation at some of his more unconventional moves in the field. His heart was warm, however, and when he dropped Charlie Barnett in the slips off Wellard he slipped the bowler a £1 note at the end of the over. There are countless stories of his endearingly oddball cricket theories. Most of them are probably true.

Meyer could be a handsome hitter. The hook was venomous; he was particularly strong on the leg-side. And in 1936 he scored a double-century against Lancashire in the last match of the season at Taunton. The innings earned him headlines and a new kind of status for someone whose county batting career had started from modest low-order. An intriguing—and not apocryphal, I'm assured—version of his undefeated 202 is revealed in Bill Andrews' autobiography. Bill claims that as soon as R.J.O. reached his century in the second innings, he turned to stumper George Duckworth.

'If I make 200, I'll subscribe £5 towards Jack Iddon's benefit.'

Somerset had by then saved the game, in any case. By an odd

coincidence, unfamiliar bowlers like Washbrook and Paynter began to appear. Duckworth even took off his pads to send down six overs—and conceded 37 runs.

It seems uncharitable to devalue the double-century. It was a popular reward for all the stimulating innovations Meyer brought to the game. Who else sorted out the field placings, while the rain lashed against the pavilion roof, by persuading hardened old pros to move around the room on their chairs as he introduced new, imaginative leg-side theories?

He was instinctively a gambler and it showed happily in his cricket. He would also pass on the occasional racing tip to his team mates as well as favoured boys at Millfield School. As a headmaster, at Millfield and later in Greece, he brought energy, drive and administrative zeal to the job. It is a pity he wasn't around more often, outrageous theories and all, for the benefit of Somerset cricket.

Record: 2,929 runs (av 28.16) 158 wickets (av 28.32)

ARTHUR MILTON
(1948–74)

At the wicket he could be infuriating. His concentration was immense and his technique wholly adequate to deal with either the fury or the wiles of the world's best bowlers. But he refused to be stirred to make alien shots or accelerate the pace simply for popular entertainment. He argued that there was skill in staying at the crease; certainly he was more infallible than most of his colleagues.

Clement Arthur Milton had impeccable judgment. He could time an innings or anticipate a leg-break. For someone so un-flurried, almost indolent by nature, he would scamper for an impossible single—and have time to lean on his bat before the wickets were broken. He never seemed to be in a hurry; yet in his deceptive way we knew he frequently was. Certainly he was as he sprinted, with such relaxed energy, down the wing for Arsenal.

61

Milton was this country's last cricket-soccer international. By 1952 he was in the first division team at Highbury and was capped against Austria after only a dozen league games. In the mid-fifties he rather surprisingly and sentimentally joined Bristol City. He made an immediate impact, helped them win promotion to the second division and drifted out of soccer.

His sporting prowess was being noted while he was still a junior at Cotham Grammar School in Bristol, seat of learning and nursery for Test cricketers. It was clear he would go on to Gloucestershire. The county could see that here was a future opening bat. 'Nothing ruffles the young so-and-so,' they used to say. He was still doing his National Service, with a severe haircut to match, when in 1948 he made his debut against Northamptonshire. By the following season his hair had grown and, in any case, he had a county cap to go on it.

Milton made 52 centuries for Gloucestershire—in his own time and own tidy, meticulous style. He would have been ashamed of an ostentatious flourish of the bat, even if the ball were soaring towards the mid-wicket boundary. Many of his runs came prettily through the covers—off the back foot. He didn't believe in giving the impression of making too much effort in any case. He scored numerous tidy off-side boundaries off the back foot because of admirable timing and the intuitive ability to elude the fielders. There were also delicate little deflections and chops and, as the players are apt to say, squirts down to third man. Maybe he had a sly sense of the dramatics as well. I remember vividly how, after flirting with our affections and patience most of the afternoon, he eventually won the game off the fourth ball of the final over. Everyone felt he should have made sure earlier; but the imperturbable, mathematically-agile Milton never doubted his ability to score the winning hit.

There's an endearing half-pace approach to life about him. One or two captains may have worried a little over this in the early days. But they came to realise it was largely a facade. He could chase a ball all the way to the boundary with a nimble willingness. The reflexes were magnificently sharp as he appeared to stroll his way through all those casual catches at slip and short-leg. He was in the Hammond class at times.

If there was a torpidity to his physical moments, his mind was keenly active. He could calculate run-targets quicker than anyone else. That and an astute tactical brain were comforting allies during his spell as captain. He could, with the same mental alertness, assess the speed of a greyhound.

Records, one feels, never meant too much to him. He scored a century against New Zealand on his Test debut and he simply steeled himself to do it. In 1968, with that dashing cavalier once with Lancashire, David Green, Milton helped to put on 315 for the first wicket at Hove: two blond heads and differing temperaments enjoying themselves relentlessly in the Sussex sunshine. I watched him in 1962 scoring an undefeated century in each innings against Kent at Bristol. If Kent tired of the sight of him, so did Somerset. The Quantocks farmers groaned whenever he ambled to the wicket.

His medium-paced bowling was not to be taken too lightly in the earlier seasons. It had a functional efficiency about it. Between overs he walked the few yards from short-leg to short-leg and philosophised to his nearest team mate. These days he rises at dawn and still philosophises engagingly—as my postman, bringing me warm summers' memories as well as the bills. Record: 30,218 runs (av 33.65) 79 wickets (45.03)

A. E. NEWTON, A. P. WICKHAM
AND H. MARTYN
(1885–1914) (1891–1907) (1901–06)

Their wicket-keeping talents are romantically dovetailed in my treasure-chest of happy Somerset hearsay. My only regret is that I have been unable, despite diligent research, to authenticate absolutely which of them turned up for a county fixture against Oxford, and 'kept' for both sides. Such haphazard arrangements and disregard for the rules were, I suspect, very much within the eccentric spirit of some of those early matches with the Universities. Somerset more than once arrived with eight or nine players. There was never too much difficulty recruiting a likely lad from among the undergraduates in the vicinity of the ground.

Arthur Newton, the Rev (later Prebendary) Archdale Wickham and Henry Martyn were all Oxford men, in fact. Sound academic pedigrees were not all they had in common. They loved their cricket and crouched behind the wicket with exceptional skill.

'The Rev' was at Oxford first, arriving by way of Marlborough. He had been born in a vicarage near Dorking and it was never envisaged that he would follow any career other than the Church. His sermons, many of them provisionally composed behind the stumps, were full of cricketing imagery. During his days as vicar of Martock he was always ready to complement the theological message of Matins with a shrewd assessment of Somerset's chances in the current match. He played his first game for the county in 1891 and juggled his appearances after that between weddings and funerals. Even as a young curate at St Stephen's, Norwich he had enjoyed serving God at the wicket as well as the altar, and was having a few impressive games for Norfolk before taking his first living in Somerset. He was Rural Dean of Ilchester from 1900 and Prebendary of Wells Cathedral from 1904. And he had some of his best matches for the county when he was past 40. When Hampshire once scored 627–7, he did not concede a bye.

Arthur Newton, born at Barton Grange, Taunton, was seven years younger than Wickham. He 'kept' for Eton and looked forward to doing the same for his native county. His first matches for Somerset came in the tentative days, before first-class status was rather grudgingly given in 1891. He went on playing for Somerset, often as the No 1 choice, and then intermittently, until 1914. There were well over 400 victims, nine of them at Lord's in 1901 when he produced the most dazzling exhibition of his career. He caught six Middlesex batsmen and stumped three more.

No stumper had sharper reflexes. He hated standing back, even to the faster bowlers. Sammy Woods could be unpredictably wayward, as well as lively. Newton intrepidly stood up to him—and that could be a hazardous occupation on some of the more unsophisticated wickets. Woods rightly had an affection for him: the extrovert Australian's first delivery for Somerset brought him a wicket with the wicket-keeper's help.

The fixture was against Warwickshire at Birmingham. Woods came puffing in with windmill flourish and Newton must momentarily have pondered the wisdom of staying his ground. The delivery was an unintentional yorker of considerable pace just outside the leg stump. Rock, the batsman, gratefully missed it; Newton miraculously stumped him. And there were many more stumpings like that. He went on tour to Australia in 1887–88 two years after enjoying a so-called cricketing jaunt with E. J. Sanders' team to America.

And then there was Henry Martyn, who played less regularly but was passionately cited by some knowledgeable greybeards as the greatest of them all. How do we measure? He was born in Devon in 1877, played for Cornwall when he was 21 and had his first matches for Somerset just after the turn of the century. Even more spectacularly, he stood up to the fastest bowlers and let surprisingly little get past him. Hundreds who never saw him play recite his skills behind the wicket and his dynamic, if joyfully irresponsible, approach to batting. Here were clearly a trio of stumpers we all pretend we watched. I like to think I was at the county ground when Newton was 'wheeled' to the wicket to play for Somerset Stragglers as a 75-year-old. Or when Martyn, with no regard for reputation, swung his bat for 130 not out against the Australians at Bath in 1905.

Records:

Newton 3061 runs (av 12.54) 415 dismissals (296 ct 119 st)
Wickham 718 runs (av 9.44) 131 dismissals (83 ct 48 st)
Martyn 2940 runs (av 24.91) 113 dismissals (78 ct 35 st)

L. C. H. PALAIRET
(1890–1909)

We grew up believing, those of us with Somerset roots, that he was the greatest of them all. Lionel Charles Hamilton Palairet, the consummate artist, the handsome batsman who shaped and sculptured every innings, did nothing at the wicket that was shoddy or even functional. Every shot—and most were off the front foot—was, our cricketing elders told us, a work of art.

It is impossible and futile to measure a Palairet with a Gimblett or a Richards. They grew from different cultures and times and pressures. Palairet had none of the private turmoil of Gimblett; Richards would have been bored by the languid, slap-happy jollity of erstwhile amateurs. We can only judge each within his era. And Palairet, whatever the England selectors thought of him, must have been a wonderful player.

He played just twice for his country. Overlooking the kind of slight that has inexplicably accompanied the history of Somerset, we can accept the biblical word of Widsen. 'Among the players of his day, there is no one better to look at. He plays in a beautiful style.'

Lionel Palairet, who for a time played alongside his slightly younger brother Richard for Somerset, had a privileged background—and a succession of capable cricket coaches enlisted by his father. He was taught not to take risks in the pursuit of batting popularity. Few of his innings gave the scorer writer's cramp. He was a stroke-maker but at his own poised pace. He could be sedate and attractive at the same time. At the crease he was a tall, authoritative figure, with an easy stance and the minimum of movement as the ball was delivered. He found it indecorous and out of character to hustle for runs and make unnatural attacking shots. Most of his were on the ground, beating the fielders because the feet were right and the timing impeccable.

Palairet was born in 1870, in Lancashire. There were obviously early links with Somerset including a spell at a Clevedon school. He went on to captain both Repton and Oxford University and he brought to his cricket a tidy, academic approach. There was an amalgam of geometry and the arts about the way he batted. Somerset knew from the time he meticulously unpacked his bag to play under Herbert Hewett they had snared a star.

West Country abounded with larger-than-life cricket personalities in those days. Palairet never competed with them for flamboyant deeds; he had no need to. The manner of the innings —and the man—was different. Extravagantly forceful cricketers like Grace and Woods acknowledged the rare artistry and ungrudgingly led the applause. And so, in 1892, everyone should have. Upstart Somerset rose to third in the table. In a match to savour at Taunton, Palairet and Hewett put on 346 for the first wicket. There are still faded prints around to substantiate it.

At times the more robust style of Hewett mildly overshadowed the phlegmatic, upright Palairet. Yet the two, so unalike, brilliantly sparked each other. One left-handed, one right, they became for a time the most consistent opening pair in the country. L.C.H. scored more than 1,300 runs in 1892; in his quiet way he enjoyed the way unfashionable Somerset were thrusting themselves into national recognition. His innings had a rare variety of strokes, although his cover boundary was the sweetest of his day. Against Hampshire in 1896 he scored 292 without giving a real chance. In 1904, away to Worcestershire, he tidily composed another double century. The run-rate was never slow—and never for a moment looked indecently flurried.

Palairet, the Poet, was a century-maker 27 times for Somerset. For a season, between Woods and Daniell, he was the captain. He was, in truth, a team-man rather than a leader. As a bowler he was useful medium-pace.

Cricket, in the pleasurable, painstaking way he played it, was a large part of his life. But he had other interests, was honorary secretary for a time of the Taunton Vale Foxhounds and carried on business as a land agent.

Record: 15,777 runs (av 33.63) 143 wickets (av 33.91)

C. W. L. PARKER
(1903–35)

Charlie Parker spoke his mind. His invective scorched its way more than 22 yards down the wicket. It was directed without fear or favour, never tempered by mealy-mouthed tact or the forelock-touching characteristics of the sycophant. He called a bat a bat—and an amateur, whatever the kaleidoscopic grandeur of the cap, just another cricketer, expected to be worth his place. The language could be strong and seldom restrained when a catch in the deep was put down. Off the field he was a kind, gentle man and he engendered considerable affection for someone basically so irascible.

Some, not only those with geographical allegiance, have claimed he was the finest left-arm spinner of the lot. In 32 years with Gloucestershire he took well over 3,000 wickets; only Rhodes and Freeman, they will remind you around Cheltenham, took more. With criminal negligence, the selectors picked him only once for England. That was at Manchester in 1921 when he bowled C. G. Macartney, the pride of New South Wales. On another occasion he was summoned to the Test arena and sensed like everyone else, except the selectors, that the pitch was made for him. He was left out, exchanged suitably contemptuous words with those who seemingly disparaged his talents and headed summarily for home.

No one will ever understand the bizarre logic of those who continued to ignore him as an England spinner. It wasn't sufficient that he trundled away to a double hat-trick against Middlesex in 1924 or that he had Don Bradman twice in that extraordinary tied match with the Australians in 1929. The record books locally are full of Charlie's feats. He would bowl with flawless skill on all types of wickets, flighting and spinning his way through the sturdiest of defences. But perhaps those who chose our national team judged Parker by his biting tongue rather than his supple fingers.

He was born at Prestbury in 1884 and first turned his arm over for the county, as a medium-paced seam bowler when he was 19. Before that he had played his club cricket for Tewkesbury and looked on himself as an allrounder. Batting prowess was less evident with Gloucestershire although there is a record of one innings of 82. He knew all the best shots, theoretically in any case, and his profound knowledge of the whole game of cricket was enjoyed and envied.

The older supporters remember graphically the Parker of faded cap and unsmiling manner. Some captains, notably Bev

Lyon, handled him better than others. His wickets were as plentiful as the apocryphal stories: every contemporary player seemed to agree that the angle of the cap became more exaggerated as the adrenalin—or anger—increased.

Charlie Parker was a beautiful bowler who intelligently schemed his successes with the ready co-operation of Hammond at slip. Theirs was a teasing, ensnaring double-act, infuriating to the victim. For a long time after he arrived at the county ground in Bristol, Parker was told to speed things up and leave the spin to George Dennett. This was not to his liking; indeed he made it plain—and there were no ambiguities in his conditions to the Gloucestershire committeemen immediately after the First War—that he was to be employed as a slow bowler or not at all. He won the argument and was soon taking 100 wickets in a season. He did it eleven times; and his wily accuracy brought him 200 wickets in five other summers.

Parker was the tough, honest professional. He reserved some of his most bewildering bowling for his benefit match against Yorkshire in 1922 at Bristol. He wheeled away brilliantly for 9–36 and had the home crowd hysterical with glee as he hit the stumps with five successive balls. The second was a no-ball but who cares? Frequently he left the Somerset innings in tatters and once took 10–79 against them. The malevolence in his bowling turned to kindly neighbourliness afterwards.

Psychologists could write a dozen books about Charlie Parker. He was a wise, fair-minded, largely self-educated man, willing to talk with as much passion about political radicalism and music as cricket. After leaving the county in 1932 he was appointed coach at Cranleigh. The boys learned how to spin the ball, to be honest to themselves and to fear no man. His philosophy was imparted with benign and disarming persuasion. The boys, like most of his fellow cricketers, loved him.
Record: 7.616 runs (av 10.41) 3,171 wickets (av 19.43)

MIKE PROCTER
(1965–   )

I met Mike Procter and Barry Richards on almost the first day they arrived at the county ground in Bristol to play a season of exploratory 2nd XI cricket for Gloucestershire. They looked like a couple of those husky campus kids, endearingly gauche, more at home in the park than at a party. The pair, fresh from their public schools, fidgeted uncomfortably for the local press photographers. In the way of outdoor boys, suddenly transported a long way from native Durban, they were not yet conversationally assured.

They were personal friends. With their similar blond hair and rugby players' shoulders they could even have passed as brothers. But when they returned to England, to play cricket here for cash, they moved in separate directions. Richards, classical batsman of the seventies, joined Hampshire. Procter, soon to establish himself as the world's best all rounder since Gary Sobers, happily chose Gloucestershire.

It is futile to evaluate their respective merits and compare one with the other. Their temperaments differed slightly and Richards eventually left Hampshire with a farewell embrace that might have been warmer. Procter, who integrated easily in Bristol, Gloucester and Cheltenham and had a generally relaxed personality off the field, stayed on—despite intermittent uncertainties about his playing future. He played mostly without a contract and preferred the professional freedoms that went with it. This occasionally brought a furrowed brow in the manager's office.

Procter had first come to this country as vice-captain of the South African Schools' party in 1963. In under three years he was making his debut for Natal in the Currie Cup competition; there were later spells with Western Province and Rhodesia. His impact on county cricket, meanwhile, was very much to the liking of the Gloucestershire committee. He officially joined the staff in 1968 and was awarded his cap in no time at all.

As a bowler he was soon a fearsome sight, if you belonged to another county. He steamed in at sprinter's pace, with an intimidatingly long run and delivery off the wrong foot to add to the batsman's accumulating neuroses. The Bristol wicket, flat and slow, offered him little. But overall he was for several seasons the fastest man around in English cricket. He encouraged amiably sadistic traits in the Gloucestershire camp followers as he hurtled, hair a-blow and shirt-tail flapping, towards a score of wickets all round the country. The supporters chorused a war-cry of lethal intent.

Procter, for his part, could be equally bellicose. He'd dig the short ball in wickedly and let go a barrage of decidedly unfriendly bouncers to convey frustration or a momentary black mood. As a captain he could be cussed and show no conciliatory leanings. That was rare, however. He is basically very good-natured, even impish. The South African has been known to bowl slow left-arm to break the monotony of the occasion. His footwear can be unorthodox. His hat-tricks, more conventionally achieved, are famous from many TV re-runs.

His batting, which now and then runs into self-inflicted problems, belongs to the great tradition of stylists. He can cover-drive as well as Hammond. He has all the shots and likes to use most of them. He is naturally forceful. In the tremendously entertaining match with Somerset at Taunton in 1979 he scored 93 in 46 minutes. There were only 23 scoring shots and eight of them were sixes. Boundary fielders at their peril flung out an arm and I still vividly picture Vic Marks rubbing bruised fingers long after a vain attempt at long-off to stop a six. That day Procter survived a difficult chance off the first ball he received. Then, shoulders hunched, he got down to business. Never has the Taunton boundary looked shorter. When he chipped a six through the open window of the players' viewing balcony, Brian Brain gingerly emerged with the ball, fluttering a white flag of surrender. There was no better-humoured West Country derby and Somerset's fielders could only stand and applaud.

Some of his best batting, statistically, was for Rhodesia. There in 1970–71 he scored six consecutive centuries to equal a world record. He played for the Rest of the World against England and made a miserable seven appearances for South

Africa before that country was outlawed for its racial policy. Procter is himself politically a liberal and sadly regrets the scope he was allowed at international level. Packer cricket was a reasonable compromise.

VIV RICHARDS
(1974–   )

He is indisputably the best in the world—as all but the blind and the bigoted will agree—when he wants to be. Never has batting looked more ludicrously easy. If his mesmeric eyes are flashing and he is hungry for runs, the bowlers may as well call it a day and go back to poker. There are a few temperamental flaws in his make-up and just occasionally he is quite contemptuous of the text-book and those well-meaning bits of advice that his father, various schoolmasters and Alf Gover once gave him. There is an utterly justifiable technical arrogance—not conceit, mind you—in the instinctive way he rejects the norm.

Isaac Vivian Alexander Richards is the nearest thing to cricketing genius since Bradman. We have the same total mastery over the bowler. The eyesight, footwork and ruthlessness of Richards are unequalled in post-war cricket. He is not an exceptionally big man but the muscles ripple and the strength is quite staggering.

Records mean virtually nothing to him, so we will not embarrass him with a catalogue of his centuries and sixes. He scored his first hundred at grammar school home in St John's, Antigua. Sixes have always come more naturally to him than singles. He resents ones and twos when fours and sixes will do. He can play a cover boundary as well as Hammond but unless bowlers are especially astute, the majority of his runs come on the leg-side. No one else in the game can pick up a perfectly pitched ball just outside his off stump and pound it so exquisitely through mid-wicket.

He will never play his finest innings for Somerset in late season or in an up-country match on tour. He's not always good at driving himself. On the big occasion, he steels himself to those powers of concentration that can impose a strain on his engagingly languid personality. He won the Gillette Cup final for Somerset with the century he promised them. He was the Player of the Series in Australia in 1979–80 because privately he didn't like some of the insults that were being thrown boorishly about. On that series he was half-fit, in considerable pain and still the most beautiful cricketing sight in the world.

Richards came to Somerset through the opportunism of the club's then vice-chairman. From 1974 he was sampling the ritualistic peculiarities of county cricket and learning how to condition himself to wickets that were often infinitely less companionable than most of those hard, dry strips in the West Indies. I was with him the day he heard for the first time he had been chosen by his country. He looked just a happy schoolboy and the Bath crowd rose to him.

He was less happy when he smashed a door at Harrogate after one of those rare and insensitive racial jibes. There were also flying splinters in the Taunton dressing rooms when he brought his faithful Jumbo bat down on the floor with a thunderous crash. That again was a release of tension and abject disappointment after failing for his side in a vital Sunday League fixture that decided the title in 1978. He is intensely emotional but such manifestations of anger surface only briefly.

Viv Richards is by nature gentle and courteous. He is extremely shy and likes to emerge from the showers long after the supporters have gone. This should convey no disaffection; he simply isn't good at handling crowds. He also runs a mile from sycophants. He prefers not to talk about the game—and especially his own contribution—once he has changed into one of the hundreds of smart, casual shirts that cram the wardrobes of his flat.

It is impossible to say how long he will continue playing. That may depend on his fitness and resistance to boredom. He talks idealistically of going home to Antigua, where he is a folk hero whatever his protestations, and starting some sort of sports centre for youngsters. Somerset can only hope he will stay yet awhile. He travels the world in a jet and comes back in the

Spring to Taunton where he likes the easy-paced life of the market town with its fish and chips and homely relationships. Richards at the crease, tapping his left toe and hunting out the tombstones in St James' churchyard, is a miraculous sight. And yet, dare I say it, his astonishing moments of fallibility, are part of the appeal. Bradman was never as fallible—and never as sweet and stirring to the eye and imagination.

R. C. ROBERTSON-GLASGOW
(1920–35)

In the years after the First World War Somerset plucked players from the universities like apples from a tree. It helped if they could pitch on a length or knew where to put a half-volley. Impeccable family connections and a row of initials to bring a fancy flourish to the scorecard were apt to clinch the scouting sortie. In the June of 1922 at the Oxford Parks there was also a double-barrelled name for the visiting John Daniell to savour. It made up for the fact that Raymond Robertson-Glasgow looked a fairly straightforward in-swing bowler. The breed generally made no visible impression on Daniell.

Somerset's skipper demonstrated his prejudices when he went in first with Jack White against Oxford. Robertson-Glasgow's bowling was to his liking. The gentle swing was predictable and Daniell was soon rather patronisingly lifting it towards the mid-wicket boundary. His over-confidence ended with a beefy hit to short square-leg. The self-protective fielder grimly held on to the ball. And the bowler was invited to have a few games for Somerset.

R. C. Robertson-Glasgow, born in 1901 in Edinburgh, would willingly have played for Scotland if anyone had ever asked him. As it was, he once nearly played for England. At least that was the bar-side information he was known to impart in a confidential aside; this delightful conversationalist and companion would at times play both his cricket and life with tongue impishly in cheek. He stayed with Somerset into the thirties and was both a popular figure and a paradox. His face was often creased in smiles and his eyes were bright and full of laughter. But, in a less gregarious role, his face clouded and he periodically suffered the pain and desperation of the manic depressive. Winter's days, away from the warmth and contact of cricketing friends, could be bleak and vacuous. He struggled through the private agonies that can so easily accompany an acute sensitivity of nature. There were breakdowns and finally he died from an overdose of drugs. His loving wife was not far away.

There were other paradoxical signs in his make-up. He was in many ways a traditionalist. He was suspicious of change and lampooned the intellectual progressives of his day. The family was full of High Tories, full of class-conscious dignity. Robertson-Glasgow himself was not particularly impressed by rank or status himself. He once wrote: 'To me, everyone is something to wonder at and I thank heaven for a taste so catholic and vulgar. I know as great a general as Julius Caesar. He's a grandfather with three orphan grandchildren. And he's not in Who's Who . . .'.

Robertson-Glasgow's qualification for Somerset is both suspect and well known. The amusingly devious Daniell worked out that there were family ties at Hinton Charterhouse and, more to the point, that a cousin, Charlie Foxcroft was the M.P. for Bath. No one complained: the miseries who objected to Len Braund's transferred allegiance had clearly handed over their bureaucratic offices by now. The county's new bowler had already acquired a new name, Crusoe. He told friends how he came by it. 'In Oxford's match with Essex I bowled Charlie McGahey with a full-toss. Back in the bowels of the pavilion he told Johnny Douglas the captain he was beaten by an old bugger he thought was dead two thousand years ago, Robinson Crusoe'.

Crusoe's first game for Somerset was frustrating stuff; he made only a nominal appearance as third-change. By 1924, however, he was beautifully on a length and getting enough movement to take 9–38 against Middlesex at Lord's. It was his best and bracketed him with the great feats of Somerset bowlers. The Lord's stint won him a place in The Gentlemen's side, opening the bowling to Hobbs and Sutcliffe. He bowled Maurice Tate for 50 and did no more than hit Sutcliffe in the midriff first ball.

Like most lower-order batsmen, Crusoe was loathe to denigrate his batting. He had been an opener at Charterhouse and once figured in a superbly defiant last-wicket stand with Peter Johnson which thrillingly added 140 runs when 217 were needed.

Apart from his cricket he was briefly a prep master, later a journalist and author. His prose was immaculate and it hummed with humour. He was a gentle poet with a classical bent but Oxford was really only a passport to a Blue. They say he would occasionally disappear into the beer-tent between wickets during the Weston festival. It is a lovely thought with which to remember him.

Record: 1,291 runs (av 14.02) 238 wickets (av 26.35)

REG SINFIELD
(1924–39)

Reg Sinfield was the first Gloucestershire professional to perform the double of 1,000 runs and 100 wickets. He did it, with plenty to spare, in 1934 and managed it again by just two runs three years later. He was an accomplished enough batsman to open the innings; and although having to take his turn after Parker and Goddard, he flighted his slow, meticulous right-arm slows with consistent success. He was the definitive good pro, liked by the other players because he was essentially a team-man and a fighter.

There were a few—well, at least two—slow Gloucestershire bowlers around who made no great effort to hide their displeasure when a catch went down. Sinfield never complained. On one of the rare afternoons when Andy Wilson let him down with both a stumping and catching chance, in the stumper's first match for the county, a kindly, almost paternal Sinfield brushed aside the intended apologies and assured Wilson a 50 per cent ratio of success was certainly acceptable to him.

Sinfield had a serious face and long chin that creased easily into smiles. Opponents always liked him and that was a significant sign of good fellowship. One Somerset professional of the pre-war era told me: 'Our matches with Gloucestershire were not exactly the height of conviviality at times. In the lunch intervals there even seemed to be a wall of silence. But dear, old Reg Sinfield was invariably the exception. He had a cheery greeting—even if he was planning to tweak you out in the first over after the break.'

The highlight of his career must have been the Cheltenham fixture against the South Africans in 1935. It was August and Gloucestershire were shuffling around near the foot of the championship table. The tourists were looking pretty invincible and no mere county seemed capable of beating them.

Dallas 'Puggy' Page, soon to die tragically in a road accident at the age of 26, was captaining Gloucestershire. And he must have been cheered by the way Sinfield, scoring confidently on the leg side in particular, made 102 out of the first innings total of 279. Hammond got a century in the second innings and the South Africans were left to score 289. At 150–3 it looked comfortably within their grasp. Sinfield had a love affair with the Cheltenham wicket and took 5–31. The South Africans were all out for 201.

Sinfield confided later: 'With Parker and Goddard doing their stuff I didn't think I had much chance of a bowl. Then I spotted a ladybird on my shirt and told the skipper I thought it might be my lucky day. I asked for just a few overs before lunch—and got Rowan and Cameron'.

Scenting victory, he rejected lunch and looked expectantly and impatiently out across the College pitch. He was first to take the ball again, flighted his canny way to three more wickets and it was all over by tea. The tourists were left surveying their tattered innings in disbelief. Cheltenham's crowd was ecstatic. There were speeches from the Mayor and the players, treated like film stars, took their sheepish bow. It was a great match for Gloucestershire—and it belonged to the unassuming Sinfield.

He had actually played his first game for the county against the South Africans, a much weaker side, at the Fry's ground in

1924. His contribution in the famous tied match with the Australians in 1930 was less dramatic: he will remember it for the way he caught Bradman at point in the first innings and ran out Ponsford for a duck in the second.

There was one Test appearance for him, against the Australians in 1938. But he might justifiably be called an England consultant. When G. O. Allen, as chairman of selectors, came to Bristol in the late fifties specifically to watch the promising David Allen, David Smith and Tony Brown ran through the opposition and the off-spinner had hardly a bowl. So Gubby Allen went into a conclave with the old firm of Messrs Sinfield, Wilson and Crapp who enthusiastically paraded the arguments for taking a chance with their young team-mate.

Sinfield was very much a kind man. He was also quite an all-rounder, as that 9–111 against Middlesex at Lord's in 1936 and those 16 well-composed centuries illustrate. The boys at Clifton College, where for a quarter of a century he was a warm-hearted coach, were visibly proud of him.

Record: 15,561 runs (av 25.89) 1,165 wickets (av 24.37)

HAROLD STEPHENSON
(1948–64)

His pads always looked slightly too big for him, even when he was batting. He shuffled around at the crease, animated and impish. He liked taking rash singles just for the hell of it. The judgment was, in fact, usually faultless and he offset the hazardous and challenging aspect of the run with the beam of visible enjoyment on his bronzed and amiable face. Batting partners, less physically able to cope with death-defying sprints, panted their way to marginal safety and looked back towards chuckling team mates in the pavilion as if to say: 'This damn Stevie's at it again'.

Stephenson arrived from Durham in 1948 on the recommendation of a North Countryman who knew that Somerset were on the look-out for Wally Luckes' successor. Taunton took to him straightaway. The headquarters had always been proud of their wicket-keepers and here they decided was another in the top-flight tradition. He did nothing wrong technically; he never snatched at the ball or mismanaged those instinctive leg-side stumpings. Best of all, he was not a show-off.

Noisy wicket keepers, greedy for victims and heady with histrionics, leave themselves open to ridicule and barracking. 'Steve' was an efficient rather than expansive operator. He was sparing in his appeals and normally confident when he shouted. Umpires liked him—and their unspoken relationship with stumpers is not uniformly cordial. Batsmen liked him, too. They heard him breathing down their necks but they sensed a chumminess rather than antipathy in that distinctive crouch. They exchanged pleasantries between deliveries.

Some would say Stephenson was the finest stumper Somerset ever had. His thousand dismissals were nearly 200 more than the next most successful of the county's wicket keepers, Luckes. When he stood up, the eyes were clear and the movement clean. The Johnny Lawrence googly might well have sent keepers as well as batsmen to distraction. Stephenson read it expertly and often allowed himself a broad grin at the little Yorkshireman's eccentricities.

In a different decade he would, very much on merit, have been the England wicket keeper. Godfrey Evans kept him out and 'Steve' had to be content with the No 2 role on tour. He must have been a popular tour member. He was liked by other players and integrated socially. But ultimately there was only one yard-stick and that was his ability behind the stumps. His catching was helped by genuine anticipation and was remarkably sharp and agile at times. He usually made it look easy. Half a dozen times, after the most brilliant of stumpings, I saw the dismissed batsmen look at him—in admiration as much as disbelief.

He used to play league cricket in Durham and he retained a lively competitiveness. That served him well during his four years as captain of Somerset. He took over from Tremlett and in four seasons led the county from 14th to 3rd in the championship table. In the memorable 1963 season Somerset lost only six matches out of 28; against Yorkshire he had nine victims.

His batting, at times from an unduly modest No 9, could be fun. He was not afraid to loft his shots and there was plenty of adventure about him. More important, he could adapt himself to the needs of the team. His great virtue, indeed, was that he was very much a team man—suicidal singles and all.

Record: 12,473 runs (av 20.01) 1,007 dismissals (698 ct 309 st)

C. L. TOWNSEND
(1893–1922)

W. H. Brain earns himself a fleeting mention in the county record books. He kept wicket for just one season, 1893. Whether or not he found favour with the hierarchy of the day, he was very much to the liking of Charles Lucas Townsend. The pair of them made a piece of history at the Cheltenham College ground against Somerset. Townsend tweaked his way to a hat-trick; all three batsmen were stumped by Brain.

Cheltenham was then even more of a friend for the spinners. And when this pleasantly precocious young man from the sixth form of Clifton College arrived and unpacked his school bag he was told: 'Just toss the ball up and don't be afraid if the Somerset batsmen try to hit you through the chapel window'.

Charlie Townsend was 16. He could bowl fastish leg-breaks without apparently having to contort his fingers. More than that, he could keep a length. He had none of the neuroses that come to so many spinners, in mid-career, when they suddenly fear that the ball is turning no longer. This young man added flight to the imparting of spin; and, as a splendid bonus, he was also a talented batsman. From what was surely a sensational county beginning, he developed into one of the memorable allrounders. When his bowling receded, his left-hand batting took over. He stayed with Gloucestershire until 1922 although appearances became very intermittent. It is not known how many more runs and wickets he might have taken. He played twice against the Australians and it might well have been more.

Townsend looked a thrilling prospect in the mid 1890s, in

Alf Dipper; Sam Cook; George Emmett; Zaheer Abbas.

Tony Brown; David Smith; triumphant Gloucestershire after their Benson and Hedges' Lord's final in 1977.

much the same way as Ian Botham did for Somerset 80 years later. He got his exams out of the way and played a full season for Gloucestershire in 1895. Here was consistent spin bowling as teasing as you would find in England at the time. Even the most experienced batsmen could not come to terms with him. He took 124 wickets and decided that cricket was better than book-learning. By 1894 he was very must established as an all-rounder. He completed the double in great style and in the bowling performance of the season took 9–48 at Lord's. Where better to parade your especial skills? The Middlesex batsmen sparred and missed: the game's elder statemen looked at one another and mentally selected Charles for next season's Australian Tests, along with W.G. and Jessop.

He was not only a good batsman, too, but an attractive one. He had the left-hander's tendency to sweep, pull and be ruthless to the leg; to be measured and refined through the covers. Masters and Old Boys from Clifton crowded the boundary when in 1899 he hit an undefeated 224 against a nonplussed Essex. His staggering tally that summer was 2,440 runs and 101 wickets. A very special cricketer had come to Gloucestershire.

The Cheltenham wicket may often have befriended the slow bowler, but not always. Townsend went back resolutely as a batsman for the 1906 Festival. The tents were up—and they were needed for only two days in the match with Worcestershire. Gloucestershire perhaps had the best of the pitch when they batted first. They were in indecent, heady haste and scored 523. Sewell hit a century. Townsend was out for 214. Then Worcestershire were bundled out twice by George Dennett, as the wicket wore. Victory by an innings—and the double century-maker never batted with greater aplomb.

There were 19 centuries by him for the county and his last was in 1909 against the Australians, yet again at Cheltenham, where the wicket over the years capriciously encouraged his beguiling leg-breaks one day and his batting the next. Some seasons after that the work kept him away almost entirely from cricket. He liked to be around for the games with Somerset, however. As late as 1920 when 'Farmer' White bowled the hapless Gloucestershire team out for 22 at Bristol before a crowd stunned to silence,

Townsend pledged to demonstrate a vengeful second innings. He went in first and disdainfully lashed 84 runs, mostly at White's expense.

Record: 7,754 runs (av 30.18) 653 wickets (av 21.92)

MAURICE TREMLETT
(1947–60)

Maurice Tremlett was the captain of Somerset from 1956–59 and I would make out an impetuous, romantic and still well-reasoned case that he was the best the county ever had. His tactical sense of the game was razor sharp. No one would argue the finer points with such undisguised affection and under-standing. In that deceptively languid way of his he never missed a nuance during the three days of the match.

He was a misunderstood and mishandled player. Somerset were not to blame—nor Tremlett himself. The MCC thought they knew best. They decided there was a surfeit of elementary mistakes in his bowling technique. Conflicting words of advice and the bowler's manual were thrown at him. Psychologically he could not absorb it all and change his ways. His head was filled with complexes; he lost his run-up, his rhythm and his line. In the end, sad and privately cynical, he gave up bowling and concentrated on the batting that brought him more than 15,000 runs and 12 centuries for his native county.

For a reason not wholly to do with logic or statistics he was one of my great favourites. Here was the handsome, blond six-footer who almost beat Middlesex on his own at Lord's, in his first county match. He bowled with untutored zest for a 5–8 spell in the second innings and then fearlessly struck the last-wicket victory runs as Horace Hazell glued himself magnificently to the other end. The Middlesex players spontaneously lined up to applaud Tremlett off the field. He was 24, with the presence and boyish style to imply an exciting England future as an allrounder. The headlines quickly grew in size and everyone seemed prematurely to be heaping praise on him. He was another Maurice Tate and the great new discovery of the post-war years. Somerset basked in the predictions. The player, unassuming and self-critical by nature, fidgeted uneasily. He knew better than most people the technical flaws in his game. He became apprehensive and it showed.

His three Test appearances were deserved. On the 1947–48 tour of the West Indies he agonised at the nets and back in his hotel room. It helped when he bowled Frank Worrall for a duck in a match with Jamaica. He returned to England and the harder he tried, the more wayward was the delivery. His mind was cluttered with kindly but confusing counsel as he ran to the wicket. His feet were wrong and the body-control minimal at the point of release. He would stand afterwards, hands on hips looking unseeingly at the ground. Crowds do not always soothe a sportsman's mental torment.

Tremlett was emotionally always close to Taunton. He went to the local Priory School, bowled happily away for teams like Rowbarton Brewery and Stoke St Mary before going into the army and did some office work at the county ground. G. O. Allen saw him playing in army matches and invited him to join Middlesex. The terms were good, the idea unthinkable.

There were inconsistencies in his batting. But he hit straight and was lovely to watch when the adrenalin was going. No one could put away a better straight driven six. I can still vividly picture the bracing of those strong shoulders as long-on and long-off moved deeper towards the ropes. Tremlett on form was made for Festival cricket: amid the evergreens and holiday makers at Weston, in particular. The short boundary at Taunton was cleared with what seemed like a golfer's chip shot.

He was not the kind who could drive himself ruthlessly and at times appeared lackadaisical. But as a cricketer he was perceptive and mentally nimble. He didn't make things easy for the opposition. He knew every visiting player's vulnerability and set the field accordingly. He used his bowlers well and, for a long time, wished he had the confidence to bring himself on again. Occasionally he offered a few token overs.

Perhaps everyone expected too much of Maurice Tremlett.

That is what comes from choosing Lord's as the stage for your dazzling debut.

Record: 16,038 runs (av 25.37) 351 wickets (av 30.63)

ARTHUR WELLARD
(1927–50)

It was umpire Alec Skelding who walked back from the pavilion to the middle at Wells in the late thirties, wagged a finger in mock rebuke at batsman Arthur Wellard and said: 'For heaven's sake, don't lose this ball. We've run out of them!'

Wellard, with not too much back-swing but plenty of beautiful, unsubtle muscle, had just belted five sixes in a row. Several balls had disappeared, apparently for ever, far out of the intimate ground and suddenly there was an embarrassing shortage of replacements. The batsman dutifully restrained himself and sheepishly settled for a few fours after that.

Wells is fundamentally a small city of cloistered calm and clerical collars. Wellard blissfully lacked the sensitivity for a matching mood. Twice he braced his sturdy shoulders to heave five consecutive balls out of the ground. He was a pragmatist and he found it easier dropping his mammoth pulls into the Tone at Taunton or some onion patch of an adjacent allotment than sparring uneasily with the likely reward of a single to third man.

Somerset has never been short of muscular hitters. Some would have recoiled if you had called them sloggers. Wellard shrugged off the description in that likeable, matter-of-fact way of his. His blows were not without science and skill. When he took guard he went through the accepted preliminaries: in his case that usually meant a brief glance to determine where deep mid-wicket and long-on were planted, and a visual reassurance that he knew where to find the shortest boundary. Not that the length of the fence from the crease ever inhibited him. He had fun at cosy Taunton no more than some of the grounds where, one suspects, opposing skippers of Machiavellian inclinations extended the ropes in deference to Wellard's arrival in town.

He was everything that schoolboys dream about. He was the England player and the blacksmith village cricketer at the same time. In fact, he was chosen only twice for England. The war years saw to that.

We all make the mistake of encapsulating Wellard's career in the memory of those mighty swipes. His strength was phenomenal, certainly, and he hit towards the clouds as if he were toying with a golf ball. I often believed that the ball would never come down. Occasionally it did with a crashing of glass. House-owners, passing car-drivers, milk delivery men and anglers all lived dangerously after he had ritualistically patted back the first three balls. But his bowling was still his greatest talent. Only J. C. White has taken more wickets for Somerset.

Wellard was born in 1903. He should by rights have played for Kent but they let him slip away. So he turned up in Somerset with a flashy suit and a bewildering facility for playing cards. In the years that followed, between taking 1,500 wickets and scoring nearly 12,000 runs, a quarter of them in sixes, he left team mates poorer from ill-advised poker schools—and cricket lovers infinitely richer from seeing him on the field. After qualifying for two years he had his first season with Somerset in 1929. He took more than 100 wickets that summer and did it seven more times. His prized hat-trick came against Leicestershire in 1937 and three times he did the double, equalling Len Braund's record.

Physically he was something of a giant, accentuated when he leapt before delivery. He could swing the ball away lethally late. And, as he particularly demonstrated in his later seasons with the county, he was an accomplished off-spinner. Somerset released him prematurely at the end. That decision came as a surprise to many of those who cherished his thrilling skills as an allrounder—and was unforgivable to boys like myself who went to shriek, like elated philistines, at his sixes as they shimmered into the afternoon sun.

Wellard was also a magnificent fielder without fear and seemingly pain. He loitered at silly-mid-off, close enough to sniff the linseed on the bat. When an off-drive was struck off the full blade he would unconcernedly throw down one of his big hands for a catch taken as simply as if he were pulling an ace from the pack. He held 400 catches for Somerset and the ball was often in his pocket as puzzled spectators searched for its scorching course towards the extra cover boundary.

He was down-to-earth, dry-humoured and an invaluable ally in any side.

Record: 12,515 runs (av 19.73) 1,614 wickets (av 24.35)

J. C. WHITE
(1909–37)

Captains come in all moods. John Cornish (Jack) White paraded no emotions. There was no visible excitement in victory and not too much outward sign of anguish in defeat. He had a placid nature and was modest about his considerable ability as a slow left-arm bowler, guileful enough to play 15 times for his country.

From 1927–31 he was Somerset's captain and he also led England three times. But in his later years, as he sat in front of the Taunton pavilion looking every bit like the untroubled Quantock farmer he basically was, few could persuade him to talk about his cricket. Personal feats embarrassed him. Cricket was for playing, not bragging about afterwards.

'Look at the clouds coming up over the hills, cock,' he would say, turning the conversation from the nostalgic moment upon which his acquired companion wanted to dwell. Jack White called everyone 'cock' with the exception of those professionals currently out of favour for a grounded catch or a preponderance of half-volleys.

He was of solid Somerset stock and had the stamina to go with it. At Adelaide, in the fourth Test of the 1928–29 series he simply kept bowling. He needed periodically to go off the field to change a shirt and gulp a draught beer but back he came, dour and willing as ever, to carry on. He bowled 124 overs altogether and took 13 wickets for 256 runs. It was a monumental stint in sweltering heat. In the end he ironically finished off the match with a couple of long-hops which 'bought' him wickets in the deep.

White's first game for Somerset was in 1909 as a 16-year-old. He didn't make much impression despite a glowing recommendation from Taunton School. By 1914, on the eve of war, he was heading the bowling averages. There were 93 wickets for him that tense summer; by the time he went back full-time to farming he had taken well over 2,000. He wasn't a spinner as such. He would wheel away all afternoon without turning the ball. But his flight was devious and cunning. There was nothing loose; he never demanded what used to be called a responsive pitch. He had the knack of finding bounce. When a delivery popped disconcertingly, Daniell was lurking at silly point for a giveaway catch. Batsmen like Hobbs and Hendren pensively held back when White was nagging away. Hammond, no great respecter of reputations, watched the beguiling flight with eagle eye.

The Chapman tour of 1928–29, which brought England the Ashes, was a personal success for White. At times he even opened the bowling with either Larwood or Tate. Usually he was brought into the attack early on. He was, in fact, a stock bowler. He slowed the runs and gave unknown complexes to the batsmen.

Back in 1921 at Worcester he took all ten wickets in an innings for 76 runs. Four times he took nine wickets, latterly before a Festival crowd at Bath intoxicated with pleasure. The whoops of delight, on this sedate, ecclesiastical ground, are still joyfully harboured in the minds of the older Bathonians. Twice, in 1929 and 1930, he did the double. It must also be said he did not like to take himself off. Who could blame him?

As a batsman he was capable of scoring 1,000 runs in a season. And he was capable of hitting 192 off the Notts attack at Taunton. He fielded well in the slips and would throw down that big, bronzed agricultural arm for some memorable stops off his own bowling.

Jack White, the farmer from Stogumber, was a hero without having to work for idolatry. He was laconic and had no dazzling personality. But his roots belonged to the Somerset hills and he made the greatest batsmen of the day grope and miss. It was a sweet and comic sight in Taunton, Bath and Weston on a summer's evening.

Record: 12,202 runs (av 18.40) 2,356 wickets (av 18.57)

S. M. J. WOODS
(1891–1910)

There is nothing more to write about Sammy Woods. The stories tumble over each other—and most of them are true, or at least in the spirit of this immensely lovable and outsized Australian. Everything about him was bountiful: his shoulders, his smile, the thrust of his bowling arm, the playful swing of his bat, his drinking capacity and the warmth of his heart.

He came over from near Sydney when he was 14 and stayed. So, in time, the West Country vowels took over. No one belonged more loyally to Bridgwater and Taunton, where at some time he lived, and the Quantocks where he hunted and, as everyone seems to know, hid his bottles of ale to refresh many a future ramble. He had no patience with conventional employment and was quickly bored by banking. It is doutbful whether he was able to save much money. But he never turned down a convivial evening, astutely lived for some time at the George Inn and was unfailingly generous with his round of drinks.

Sammy Woods was the most gregarious sportsmen of his day. While 'W.G.' was inclined to drink his whisky amid a coterie of affluent amateurs, Woods was quite indiscriminate in his socialising. If there was something on in Taunton, he was there. When the Fair arrived, he climbed roguishly into the ring. He skittled with rosy-faced zeal and sang, very acceptably in tune, at the village harvest homes. He was extrovert, noisy and offended no one. He came from a big family and always wanted to be surrounded by friends. There was no lack of these. He was not perhaps the most intellectual product of Cambridge but his conversation, which carried a sting and a colourful spectrum of adjectives to complement the natural bonhomie, instantly attracted a captive audience, whether on a beagling sortie, at Taunton cattle market or as he sprawled on the grass between wickets. Before a game he would take a brisk walk around the town. Fellow cricketers, his willing companions, were left incredulous at his knowledge of local industry and custom and a sincere acquaintanceship with nearly everyone he met in Taunton's back streets.

Woods had to be a sportsman. He was beautifully built with shoulder and chest muscles made for physical contact. For a long time, as he put on weight to 15 stone, there was no superfluous flesh. He ran well for a big man. He shoved zestfully as a rugby wing forward and was good enough to play for England. They say he happily chatted away to himself and was fearless in the mauls. He certainly enjoyed the sing-song that followed as much as the match itself.

It is as a cricketer, however, that Somerset remembers him. He was a tall, fast bowler, altogether too fiery for the Oxford batsmen during his Varsity days. The Australians came over in 1888 and reasonably claimed him as one of theirs. He played in three Tests for them. Later he was to play for England. The apparently contrasting loyalties amused him. He was never a great man for boundaries, unless they were those of Somerset.

Woods captained the county for a dozen years, from 1894–1906 although he pretended he could not remember how long. During that time he once belted the Sussex attack for 215 at Hove. 'Nice air round here, me old dear. Bracing,' he said as he came off the field.

As a captain he led by example. He bowled his heart out, consistently hostile and mostly accurate. He batted with good-natured aggression and considerable skill. Imprudent hooks and pulls brought banter with a sighing stumper. Imprudent or not, he made 18 centuries for Somerset.

He played 20 years for the county, excelled in some great wins against the almost invincible Yorkshiremen and placed himself alongside the West Country's great allrounders. Eventually the hips let him down. He continued to play, with a limp and a digger grin, for the local farmers. He still recommended a massage of high-proof spirits for cramp. The arthritis got worse and the style less boisterous. Sammy Woods died aged 62 and there will never be another one.

Record: 12,657 runs (av 25.06) 557 wickets (av 24.25)

TOM YOUNG
(1911–33)

Cricket is a felicitous leveller and the man with the broad shoulders and bulging biceps is not necessarily the boldest stroke-maker. Tom Young often looked a frail and pallid figure on the field. He fought a losing battle with ill-health and was sadly dead by the age of 45. But at the crease he summoned up a deceptive strength and was always disinclined to score slowly.

Tom, who was born and buried at Bath, played much of his cricket for Somerset between 1922–1933 as a high-order or opening batsman. His runs—and there were plenty of them—came most readily from off side shots. His square-cut was genuinely envied; there was a granite quality to the wrists as if to contradict a modest stature and slightly dour demeanour. Like so many Somerset batsmen before and since he relished risks. Back in the pavilion, Jack White was occasionally left shaking his head reprimandingly as an early wicket had been over generously donated to the opposing away-swinger. But Young was a batsman with a quiet sense of adventure and you would never change him.

His ill health and labouring lungs could be largely traced to his four years, mostly in France, during the First World War. He was seldom fully fit but courageously disguised the physical handicap. Pluck, indeed, was the hallmark of the man. It showed in the unflinching way he stood up to bowlers like Larwood and Voce; it showed in the patently painful way he grimly held on to a catch from F. T. Mann at Lord's in 1927 when the ball threatened to bore through the fielder's stomach and still carry on first-bounce to the boundary. He had a wry kind of humour. After making 32 against Notts and Larwood, he intrigued a raw Bill Andrews by keeping on his pads.

'Wh-what's the idea then, Tom?'

'Waste of time taking 'em off, son. We'll soon be bloody well in again.'

Slow bowlers didn't have so much scope when White was

around. Rather belatedly, Somerset discovered Young's prowess as an off-spinner. He did not need a particularly responsive wicket: he could pop on a length straight away and stay there, with enough gentle turn to command respect. It was 1930, however, before he started to wheel away. He expressed his gratitude by taking more than 70 wickets in the season and was probably surprised to find he ended up sixth in the national averages. Young kept taking wickets in the final summers of his cruelly terminated career. Against Derbyshire his 8–30 earned him the kind of headlines he had never imagined; it was a good match for him as he scored 63 and 70.

He wondered how he would fare against the Australians or even if he would get a bowl. Don Bradman hit a century and was then dismissed by Young. Not once did Bradman waver in his significant respect for the off-spinner. The Australians made 360 in that innings and Young—for seven years not considered talented enough to send down more than a token over—took five wickets for 70 runs.

Young ranks with Somerset's true allrounders. He hit eleven centuries for the county, usually in brisk fashion although occasionally he would draw back reluctantly into extreme caution at the bidding of his captain. As a bowler his unspectacular reliability and accuracy were a bonus for any side. In his last summer, when he was looking frailer than ever, everyone tried to will him to the double. He finished with 90 wickets and 951 runs. The lungs let him down, not the heart.

Record: 13,081 runs (av 25.40) 388 wickets (av 25.58)

ZAHEER ABBAS
(1972–   )

I have seen him score fifties with the speed of a slogger. But not once did he look as though he was in a hurry. Muscular heaves and improvised, unnatural blows from the bat, intended to banish the ball to the next county at least, make him shudder. There is nothing remotely ugly about his batting.

Zaheer Abbas has been one of the most beautiful stroke-makers of the seventies. Not all the time, mind you. He seemed painfully ill-equipped to cope with many of our county wickets when he followed Sadiq Mohammad, his Pakistan team mate, to Gloucestershire in 1972. He did not enjoy the constant need to re-adapt from three-day to one-day cricket. Occasionally he looked jaded from the sheer volume of his matches for twelve months of the year.

We shall all remember him for his 1976 batting. Runs simply proliferated from a bat which he handled with the delicate affection more often reserved for a violin. The bat never looked like a blunt instrument in his hands; it was a finely fashioned piece of equipment that brought music and aesthetic joys. Bowlers could not bowl him out in that warm summer. He carried on one innings after the other as though he had no home to go to in between. The concentration was enviable, the range of purist strokes even more. His 2,554 runs were the most made in an English season for 15 years.

'Zed', as everyone knows him, is an alphabetical contradiction. His name should be at the other end of the scale. He stands with the most handsome of the post-war stroke makers. His county captain, Tony Brown, used to bracket him with the two Richards, Barry and Vivian. There is a slightly odd flourish to the Zaheer backlift and absolutely nothing else ostentatious about him. His bats with his shirt sleeves buttoned at the wrist and still looks, as I wrote some years ago, like an innocent, well-starched choirboy.

Zaheer was never given a day's coaching in his life. His father emphasised the virtues of study so he got night school and the text books out of the way before he turned seriously to cricket. No one showed him how to hit the ball; he learned it from the Pakistan and visiting stars he watched with such impatient pleasure. At Karachi in 1969 he was rather uncharitably given out for hitting the ball twice in a match for Pakistan International Airways. The bizarre incident has lived with him, via the record books, and he no longer courts danger with pedantic umpires.

He's quiet, courteous, approachable. He sits down and

rationalises an unexpected loss of form or a newly acquired habit which could bring a flaw to his batting. He graciously takes a compliment but effusive, back-slapping praise embarrasses him. He's deliberate and level-headed in his views, whether they are about the family construction business at home or his involvement with Kerry Packer.

Zaheer was scoring four centuries in a row as long ago as 1970. Twice, amid the harvest of his 1976 runs, he hit a double and single century in the same match, at the Oval and Canterbury. He did the same, without being dismissed, at Cheltenham the following year. I watched and sympathised with the exasperated Sussex bowlers. He has shown magnificent—and disappointing—form for his country.

My abiding memory belongs to Taunton in the August of 1979. It was the most marvellous match between the two West Country counties I have ever seen. Centuries were bewilderingly thick on the ground. And Zaheer's was the best of them all.

This elegant world-class batsman, who openly abhors a hearty old-fashioned slog when the feet are wrong and the blade is swished across the line of the ball, scored 147 in 146 minutes in that game. He did it in 40 overs and in that eventful time hit nine sixes and 11 fours. Poor Dennis Breakwell, whose only crime was to pitch on a length, conceded 30 in one over to Zaheer. One of those sixes passed far over the stand and landed in the runner beans. Gloucestershire, it may be imagined, needed runs quickly on this third day. Yet not once did this neat, well-manicured Pakistan batsman look uncharacteristically aggressive and intent on catching the next train back to Bristol.

It was a rare treat. Dynamic hitting, made for the delirious delight of the spectators and the despair of runner bean growers, can still be an art form.

Shorter Notices

West Country county cricket is peopled by famous names—players renowned for their personalities as well as their sheer talent. On the following pages I complete my 'personal century'. The shorter biographical treatment of these cricketers is not intended in any way to reflect either less skill or influence. The admiration and affection is just as great.

BILL ANDREWS (1930–47) goes into any gallery of Somerset's most colourful players. We could write a book about him; he already has done that with memorable success. He had perhaps the best bowling action of his time, the best handwriting and indisputably the best fund of stories, all told without malice.

Twice he achieved the double and in 1937 against Surrey he did the hat-trick. Only the war, surely, prevented his playing for England; he has a suspicion that Wally Hammond vetoed his chances before that. He and Wellard were a marvellous pair to open the bowling; then in a borrowed pair of boots he—and Buse—bowled out the Indians before lunch at Taunton. His impetuous nature is part of his charm and Somerset has never had a more wholehearted supporter. After finishing as a player, he proved himself a sound coach and insatiable discoverer of talent.

Record: 768 wickets (av 23.37) 4,999 runs (av 15.77)

COLIN ATKINSON (1960–67) is a Yorkshireman and a fighter. It showed in his cricket when he willed himself to be a better player than perhaps he was. His application was prodigious: when he walked out with England's captain Colin Cowdrey to toss up in the 1967 Gillette final, he knew there was a gulf between them in ability. 'But I told myself I'd try twice as hard.' Before coming to Somerset to teach at Millfield (he's now the headmaster) he had graduated in English at Durham and taken a post-graduate course in psychology, partly subsidised by playing Saturday afternoon cricket as a pro in Northumberland.

Somerset took to him—his lively leg spinners, his brilliant fielding in the covers and a pleasant personality. His batting, too, could at times be intelligent and defiant. When arthritis stopped his spinners, he switched to seam bowling. As a captain he was competitive and not wholly without controversy. A calculated 'crawl' against Gloucestershire at Bristol led to noisy scenes and an unrepentant Atkinson said: 'I had a duty to 15 other counties not to give away 10 points.' His great regret was that his final appearance at Lord's, in the final, did not bring victory. But he stayed close to Somerset and became a conscientious president.

Record: 3,772 runs (av 19.05) 190 wickets (av 31.02)

JACK BOARD (1891–1914) was a nimble, natural wicket keeper who could also bat. His name was mentioned with especial endearment around Bristol in 1900 after he had gone down to Taunton and taken a double-century off Sammy Woods & Co at Bank Holiday time. 'WG', whose warmth for the professionals was not exactly all-embracing, had given Board his first chance and liked to cite the fact as evidence of sound judgement. The wicket keeper had been a poorly paid gardener before becoming no doubt a poorly paid professional. But he was willingly lured away from the onion patch in 1891 to play for the South against the North. He went with £2 from Mrs Grace and detailed instructions on which train to catch for Lord's. In the years that followed 'WG' more than once had him throwing down his stumper's gloves to chase the ball unavailingly to the square-leg boundary. He complemented 'the accepted sweat of the pro' by a magnificent record of catching and stumping until 1914. There was one double century, seven centuries and six appearances for his country.

Record: 13,109 runs (av 19.22) Dismissals 1,013 (312 stumpings and 701 catches)

TONY BROWN (1953–77) took over from Grahame Parker as Gloucestershire's second secretary-manager. He was made for

Tom Graveney—hooking; Gilbert Jessop—crouching; Ron Nicholls, John Mortimore and Arthur Milton.

Jack Crapp, the quiet, popular Cornishman; Wally Hammond, towards the end of a great career; Mike Procter, in free-scoring mood.

the job; he was clear-headed, positive, strong-minded and *au fait* with the present needs of the game, in terms of sponsorship and media involvement. He relished responsibility—and that was what made him a notable captain of the county. As a skipper he led by example in the splendid 1973 Gillette Cup win over Sussex. He sent towering sixes into the Mound Stand at Lord's at the right time and won the Man of the Match award. It was said to be primarily as a batsman that he joined the staff in 1953 and had George Emmett nodding approvingly. An all-rounder he was, but in truth the batting receded and the controlled medium-paced swing bowling surfaced. There was a hat-trick against Glamorgan at Swansea and long before that, 7–11 against Yorkshire when they had a moan about the light. His fielding was ubiquitous and often outstanding: he went into the record books with seven catches in an innings on a wet Trent Bridge day. At some time or other he played rugby at full back and soccer at centre forward.

Record: 1,223 wickets (av 25.47) 12,684 runs (av 18.14)

J. A. BUSH (1870–90) was a close personal friend of W. G. Grace and that, apart from any other consideration, would have ensured him a place in the Gloucestershire XI. It helped that he was also well worth his place. He was the county's first recognised wicket keeper, a big man with bushy black whiskers, who looked slightly unnatural, because of his height (well over 6 ft) behind the stumps. But his hands were sure and his appeal autocratically sonorous. Arthur Bush was born in India and seemed to be of independent means. There was always time for a game of cricket—or even the occasional tour. He was 'WGs' best man, a sign of particularly warm friendship, and then went off with The Champion, new wife Agnes, Fred Grace and W. R. Gilbert on what everyone jocularly called 'the honeymoon tour' of 1873 to Australia. He played his early cricket at Clifton, batted modestly as a left-hander and took off the stumper's gloves long enough to bowl 34 overs.

Record: 1,181 runs (av 8.09) 267 dismissals (80 stumpings and 187 catches)

J. H. CAMERON (1932–47), son of a West Indian doctor who himself came to England as a member of the tour team in 1906, had two sensational peaks in a career which could never live up to them. He'd been showing some lively (and amusing) form as a googly bowler at Taunton School and was picked to play in the public schools' showcase at Lord's. He played for The Rest, no-one knew what to make of him and he took all ten wickets for 49 in the first innings. Somerset's officials chased around to Taunton School and signed the young man. He made his debut for them and his expansive googlies were painfully expensive. But he did top the batting averages in 1933 and made one undefeated century. He went up to Cambridge where, as with Somerset (two centuries in 1937) his bowling was less impressive than his batting. Then, in 1939, came his other memorable feat. He came over as vice-captain of the West Indies touring side and in the first Test quickly dismissed Gimblett, Hammond and Paynter.
Record: 1,373 runs (av 18.55) 45 wickets (av 43.66)

CECIL CHARLES COWPER CASE (1925–35), from his days at King's School, Bruton, decided there were virtues in batting, other than those associated with the flamboyant flashing of the bat. He left other Somerset men to over-work the scorers and hog the headlines. 'CCC' or 'Box' Case was born in 1895 and played his first match for Somerset when he was 30. Impatient supporters never bothered him. His shots were at times unorthodox and the dour dependability he brought to an often self-destructive batting side was more valuable than perhaps it appeared at the time. His first century, in 1927, was at the expense of Gloucestershire and his best was reserved with a sense of occasion for the Oval in 1931. 'Box' scored his 1,000 runs several times and this bachelor retired from the game in 1935.
Record: 8,515 runs (av 22.17)

BRIAN CLOSE (1971–77) arrived at Taunton, installed himself at the 'Crown and Sceptre' and showed Somerset how to play the Yorkshire way. That meant more steel at the wicket and less dreaming in the field. He chased a few of the younger professionals a bit but was a popular skipper. His career was often contentious and by the time he was receiving pleading overtures by phone from Bill Andrews he'd had enough of Yorkshire cricket. He wasn't always loved by the English hierarchy, of course, though he was the youngest cricketer ever to play for this country. Time has happily healed the rift and he's now part of the selectors' 'establishment' himself.

His courage at the crease was legendary; so it was at short leg, where vicious pulls bounced off his head and he called for midwicket to hold the catch. He could battle or sweep joyfully himself—and was then a gregarious and jocular companion, surrounded by West Country accents, back at the bar. His ruggedness was largely a myth. He was basically sentimental, gambled with only modest success (despite sprints to the press tent at Festival time for a bet on inside information) and was nearly as impressive in the one-day games—whatever his protestations—as in 'cricket proper'.

Somerset Record: 7,567 runs (av 39.41) 74 wickets (av 34.94) 140 catches

BEAUMONT CRANFIELD (1897–1908) was dead by the age of 35 after an attack of pneumonia. His health had never been sturdy; but he encapsulated so much genuine talent as a slow left-arm spinner into that brief cricketing career. He didn't simply flight the ball. He wrapped it inside his fingers and spun it teasingly. At times, especially towards the end, he was embarrassingly expensive. At his most beguiling he was selected for the MCC against the Australians at Lord's in 1902. Often he partnered Braund and Somerset never had a more mischievous pair of tweakers. The two of them journeyed to Scarborough to play for the MCC against Yorkshire and between them took all but one of the wickets. 'Craney', who started by deputising for Tyler, was small, popular and often a match-winner. He also once got to within five runs of making a century.

Record: 563 wickets (av 24.43)

MONTY CRANFIELD (1934–51) was the off-spinner who never complained. He might have, reasonably enough. He came down from Lancashire as Tom Goddard's deputy—and that was more or less what he remained. Perhaps he chose the wrong county, as he must have mused retrospectively. Certainly he spun the ball sufficiently to walk into one or two other sides. He liked Gloucestershire, joked his way through all the frustrations and was a fine influence in the changing rooms. In the tense and vital match in Bradford in 1947, when Yorkshire were beaten, Cranfield was 12th man. Ever a practical joker, he deliberately dropped an old tin tray behind a line of pensive home players waiting to bat. Such levity was not too well received. But he was so anxious himself on the third day that he couldn't watch, and spectator Eddie Paynter made an unlikely appearance as Gloucestershire's sub. Monty was a pale, perky team-man who, even when he was included, seemed to spend a painfully long time running round the outfield while Goddard and Cook maintained their marathon spells.

Record: 233 wickets (av 32.92)

JACK CRAPP (1936–56) had the distinction of being Gloucestershire's first professional skipper. He was not dynamic or madly imaginative; but he possessed Cornish commonsense and was liked by his players. In fact, he was the cricketer everyone liked—a warmth extended to him during his days, later, as a respected Test match umpire. Wally Hammond soon noted the virtues of this dependable left-hander. In return, Crapp scored his maiden century and more than 1,000 runs in his first season. His tally of centuries before he retired was 36, all of them tidy and free of fancy strokes.

Against the Australians at Bristol in 1948 he intelligently built an innings of 100 not out. Keith Miller, generous as ever, said: 'Well done, Jack. But watch your head in the Test.' The modest Cornishman had won a place in the England side—and despite the Miller warning he walked into a Lindwall bouncer. He bravely refused to leave the crease. There were seven Test matches for him. In a lengthy career he snapped up catches at first slip as conscientiously as he propped the middle-order of many a sagging innings.

Record: 22,195 runs (av 34.84)

100

J. J. FERRIS (1892–95) was one of those outward-going Aussies who came over to play against England and was persuaded to stay. He was probably ensnared by the Grace scouting network. His Test appearances for Australia were clinched on the strength of his left-arm bowling. But he also fancied his batting and in his relatively brief stay with Gloucestershire he watched The Champion at close quarters and noticeably improved his own modest technique. 'WG' paid him the compliment of walking to the wicket with him as an opener (even if Grace monopolised the strike). Ferris hit his only century for Gloucestershire, in his second season, against Brighton at Hove.

His Test career against England started in 1886 and he puzzled a few of the game's bureaucrats by playing once for England on a tour of South Africa. He was a self-confident amateur who made a definite impact as he passed through the West Country. Ferris fought with the Imperial Light Horse in the Boer War and five years after leaving Gloucestershire he was dead.

Record: 1,845 runs (av 17.41) 130 wickets (26.52)

GERALD FOWLER (1888–1903) and W. H. FOWLER (1880–85) were both century makers for Somerset in the very early days, so they had more than a name in common. Gerald came by way of Oxford and opened the innings for the county in their first match of recognised senior status (1891). It was a wet Whitsun but between the showers, Fowler and Hewett made half their side's runs. Before that he'd done valuable pioneering and administrative work as Treasurer for Somerset—and justifiably reminded friends that he bowled Sammy Woods in the 1888 Varsity match. He once went to Lodway and scored 173 out of Somerset's total of 435 in less than three hours.

Away from the liberties of village cricket, he still put on 205 with Palairet for the first wicket against Gloucestershire in 1895. As for 'WH', his claim to fame was his batting—not the majesty of his shots but the the distance they travelled. At Lord's against MCC and Ground, he hit one ball 157 yards (and took a hat-trick). At Gloucester, also in 1882, he carted a delivery from

W. G. Grace for 154 yards. It was no way to win a friendship with The Champion.
Records: Gerald 3,571 runs (av 16.84) W.H. 905 runs (18.49)

KEN GRAVENEY (1947–64) qualifies for a mention in the list of 'best cricket quotes'. After brilliantly taking all ten wickets against Derbyshire at Chesterfield in 1949, he gazed incredulously at the famous spire. 'And I don't believe that bloody spire is crooked, either!' He'd caught Derby on a green wicket, swinging the ball away with devastating effect. Ken had been a Royal Marine commando. He brought brother Tom to Gloucestershire and had no complaints at all in being inevitably overshadowed by him in the years that followed. Then he worked tirelessly to persuade Tom to stay, at the time of the rumpus. Ken's own career was seriously affected by back trouble but he gamely returned, as a caretaker skipper, for the 1963 and 1964 seasons. Tom Pugh had been controversially in charge and there was need for strength and experience at the top. The Graveney link with Gloucestershire happily goes on. Son David is in the team, of course, and Dad is the chairman.
Record: 170 wickets (av 27.67)

DAVID GREEN (1968–71) was released by Lancashire in 1967 and Gloucestershire made a timely capture. He came in the shape and style of Charlie Barnett. He was an opening bat with a cavalier approach. The shine of the new ball never noticeably bothered him and he aimed to win the psychological battle with the bowlers from the first over. His departure from Lancashire was a surprise to outsiders; after all he had made 1,000 runs for them in his first season and was vice-captain by the mid-60s. From days at Manchester Grammar School and Oxford, his batting promise was an exciting talking point. Some argued he was just as good at rugby. There were many notable, crisp-scoring innings for Gloucestershire including a brilliant 233 in an opening stand with Milton (122) after Sussex had put them in at Hove in 1968.
Record: 4,703 runs (av 32.43)

CHRIS GREETHAM (1957–66) wins his place in this book, it might be argued, for sartorial style. He was county cricket's smartest dresser in his day and still looked rather like a good-looking young matinee idol after a scorching day in the field. Links with the film industry and showbiz are not completely misplaced. He was a film extra (as well as a diamond sorter and a schoolteacher). He was also a very competent cricket all-rounder. As a medium-paced bowler he needed to be used intelligently and sparingly and Maurice Tremlett, in particular, realised this. He developed the craft of seam bowler, became very tidy and would have been even more of an asset in the one-day cricket of the Seventies and later. His batting matched his appearance: classy, eye-catching and wholly personable. The cover drive was a beauty and his highest score of 151 not out was, too.

Record: 6,723 runs (av 21.97) 195 wickets (28.35)

BILL GRESWELL (1908–30) turned up as an 18-year-old from Repton and immediately had the wiseacres whistling. It wasn't just the way he could swing the ball without really trying: he managed it so late. He was certainly one of the best exponents of in-swing. Repeatedly he took experienced batsmen by surprise—and there was Pill's George Hunt gobbling up a relatively simple catch at short leg. Ancient Westonians still talk animatedly of the day Greswell took 9-62 at the expense of bamboozled Hampshire at Clarence Park. His span with Somerset was a lengthy one but the war came out of it and then there were his business commitments in Ceylon. He came from West Somerset, that corner which reared Gimblett and White. By 1911 he was taking 100 wickets. There was something of a regular comeback by him in 1922 when he captured 77 wickets and revealed that he could still move the ball as wickedly as ever. It's pointless now to ponder how much more successful he might have been. He was a useful batsman and made one century of which he was inordinately proud.

Record: 2,416 runs (15.48) 454 wickets (av 21.56)

WALTER COOTE HEDLEY (1892–1904) was a colonel in the British Army, who went off to South Africa to do his fighting. He was a military man first but cricket was his therapy and he played it well. It therefore seems slightly churlish to cite his principal claim to fame in the context of Somerset C.C.: he was supposed to be 'a chucker'. His action raised eyebrows and led to committee meetings. He was one of several of his era who were said to have suspect action. Maybe Yorkshire complained after he'd taken 14-70 against them at Taunton in 1895. He bowled quickish medium-pace and could come up with timely runs, often made by very acceptable stroke-play. Colonel Hedley was born at Taunton, educated at Marlborough and was understood to have had some early games for Kent, maybe during a temporary posting. There was one century in his 84 matches for Somerset.

Record: 2,395 runs (av 18.14) 254 wickets (20.77)

VERNON HILL (1891–1912) was one of Somerset's many Oxford men in the early days. He fancied his batting sufficiently for the occasional wager. When he played in the 1892 Varsity match, he ran a book among his fellow undergraduates and backed himself to make both 50 and a full century. With hand on heart (and figuratively on wallet) he cracked a few early boundaries to give himself confidence and ended with 114. He was the hero of the match—and doubtless collected. In truth, his schoolboy and University form were not quite sustained in the service of Somerset. He was at times overshadowed, understandably enough, by Palairet and Woods. Once in 1898, however, he swung an indiscreet and vastly entertaining bat with Sammy—and the two put on 240 for the seventh wicket against Kent at Taunton. His approach was seldom dour, although he never quite sorted out a few technical shortcomings at the crease.

Record: 3,842 (av 19.21)

HARRY HUGGINS (1901–21) was, like Fred Roberts, Bill Murch and other professionals of that era, a willing worker. A talented one, too: when Sussex came to Bristol in 1904, he was

almost unplayable. He bowled away on a length and finished with 9-34. Sussex had every reason to fear him; two years earlier he went to Hove and took 7-17. He was a reliable rather than spectacular bowler on the whole. After Roberts had retired and gone back to his pub full-time, 'Huggy' usually found himself bowling at one end and Dennett the other. It was a penetrative pairing, never to be under-estimated. He brought a conscientious approach to his cricket, prided himself on his batting and hunted for an elusive hundred. The nearest he came was 92 and everyone was willing him to succeed when he was out.
Record: 4,375 runs (av 14.43) 584 wickets (29.03)

PETER RANDALL JOHNSON (1901–27) was, in any context, one of the great stylists of Somerset cricket. It was the county's misfortune that he also had work to do—unlike many of the amateurs of his day—and sport had to remain an indulgence to be enjoyed sparingly. He was a natural batsman: the feet were always right, while the wrists lent an elegance to nearly every stroke. Messrs Warner and Douglas would have liked him to go with them to Australia but after agonising over such a flattering overture he realised that he had to put his business commitments first. Not only was he one of Somerset's most graceful batsmen but he was also one of the game's nattiest dressers. The late Christopher Hollis used to recall Johnson turning up for a match in top hat and morning coat. P. R. Johnson was a man of infinite style on or off the field.
Record: 10,202 runs (av. 25.82)

MERVYN KITCHEN (1960–79) had the rolling gait of a sailor and latterly the comfortable build of a Somerset farmer. He was, in fact, as authentically 'Somerset' as Nailsea and Flax Bourton in their pre-Avon days. That was where he used to play his village cricket as a 15-year-old: a left hander with one eye conveniently on survival and the other on the mid-wicket boundary. He was impressive rather than stylish, although he could always whack the ball expertly through the covers. He could also be the man for a crisis, dogged and gutsy, whether in the middle of the order or opening the innings. Once, in the mid-70's, he left cricket to look for a career outside. The game emotionally drew him back and he acknowledged that he had made a mistake.

Record: 15,213 runs (av 26.41)

GEORGE LAMBERT (1938–57) was not the most towering pace bowler of his day by any means—but he had the knack of bouncing the ball. It put him in the running for a trip to Australia. Such heady recognition never quite reached him. His value to the county seemed to vary and eventually rather tailed away; he was always, however, a lively in-swing bowler who shared many a new ball with Colin Scott, with whom he also shared many a hotel room on away trips, and cricketing anecdotes.

Lambert came from Paddington and retained a Londoner's sense of humour. He went to Lord's and might have been expected to join Middlesex. G. O. Allen viewed him as a promising young bowler but Gloucestershire pounced, it appears, when Gubby was away. His batting was not to be underestimated and two years before he left the county he scored an undefeated maiden century at Worcester. Colleagues tell of the day at Bristol when he was barracked by three schoolboys for playing defensively almost as soon as he reached the wicket. He queried such ungenerous response—and discovered they were his own children. Lambert later had a spell as coach to Somerset, a rare example of switched allegiance in the West Country.

Record: 6,288 runs (av 15.01) 908 wickets (28.45)

BRIAN LANGFORD (1953–74) made his debut at Bath, where the wicket can be capricious and a good friend to the spinner. In the three matches there, at Festival time, he took 26 wickets. It was a marvellous way to arrive. But for the next 21 years he kept on gently spinning the ball and maintaining a length. Only White and Wellard have captured more wickets for Somerset. There were a number of memorable performances from him: an 8-96 in that sensational Bath opening, and then

9-26 against Lancashire on a drying wicket at Weston-super-Mare five years later.

He followed Roy Kerslake as captain and did a competent job. Where once he delighted the Weston supporters, he upset them in 1970 when he decided to bat on after tea against Tom Graveney's Worcestershire. The club flag was lowered to half-mast and other demonstrators walked in front of the sight-screens. 'I was never in a position to declare—the pitch was too good,' he said to placate his critics. Langford could make timely runs late in the order.

Record: 1,390 wickets (av 24.89)

JOHNNIE LAWRENCE (1946–55) didn't seem much taller than the stumps. He specialised in leg-breaks and googlies, and bringing gentle chuckles to all those who enjoyed an afternoon of old-fashioned magical entertainment (sleight-of-hand variety) and a few impish tumbles at short leg as a bonus. He was a Yorkshireman and could bat like one when the fighting fibre was needed. Once he played 2nd XI cricket for his native county; later he took 6-29 against them at Harrogate and the hat-trick at their expense in Taunton during his final season for Somerset.

He came to the West Country by way of Bradford League and endeared himself to Somerset because of his happy dispo-sition—quite part from his clever and often bewildering bowling. In his first season he scored 968 runs and picked up 66 cunning wickets; by 1949 he was taking 100 wickets. Johnnie was well served by his wicket keepers. He, in turn, served the county well—whether pouncing for catches close to the stumps, puzzling the best batsmen or being a good influence in the changing rooms.

Record: 9,183 runs (av 20.49) 798 wickets (24.97)

FRANK LEE (1929–47) was born at Marylebone and so really had to be a cricketer, like brothers Jack and Harry. He arrived to qualify for Somerset in 1925 and by 1929 was a regular member of the side. That was when he scored his first county hundred, against Hampshire. The quiet, painstaking progress continued. In 1931 he was second in the batting averages, in

1932 he figured in a memorable first-wicket stand of 234 with brother Jack, and in 1933 he topped 1,000 runs for the first time. Frank was a diligent left-hand bat who refused to be hustled or forced into alien shots. He was an ideal opening partner for Gimblett, the necessary sheet anchor and restorer of sanity when his teammate was sadistically over-working the scorers. The two had a valued affinity at the wicket and they could be the despair of new-ball bowlers, whatever their reputations. With 23 Somerset centuries behind him, he retired and moved with distinction onto the umpire's list. He had sound judgment to complement a friendly nature.

Record: 15,252 runs (av 27.98)

ALBERT LEWIS (1899–1914) was in spirit an authentic Somerset lad—although born on the fringe of Bristol—and could easily have made a career for himself as a soccer player. Not only that: he was the best billiards player in Taunton. Recurring injuries eventually caused him reluctantly to retire from cricket while he was still in his mid-30s but he continued to talk warmly of his favourite game behind the counter in his sports outfitter's shop. He played in distinguished company, of course.

Once, at Taunton in 1901, he refused to be overshadowed by the beautifully poised Palairet and their opening stand was worth 258. He, Braund and Robson were the only three regular pros in the years leading up to the First War. Lewis retired with one ambition unfulfilled. He hoped just once to score a century in each innings; against Hampshire at Taunton he scored 101 and . . . 97. Aptly in his benefit season he hit the Kent bowlers for an undefeated 201. His bowling was mostly straight and tight but he was also capable of swinging the ball considerably in humid conditions.

Record: 7,633 runs (av 21.32) 513 wickets (av 23.18)

TOM LOWRY (1921–24) was a New Zealander who played seven times for his country and just under 50 matches for Somerset. He was a forcing bat, a modest wicket keeper and a colourful member of the side. His vocabulary was amusingly odd and at times pointed, his batting non-conformist rather than stylish and he liked to wear an old homburg when he went out to the crease.

He was born in 1898 and graduated, more or less, from Christ's College, Christchurch to Cambridge, where he got a Blue in 1923 without distinguishing himself as a batsmen. The following year he captained the University. Somerset liked the look of him and he qualified by residence for them. His native loyalties were suspect. He played for New Zealand against England and in 1922–23 toured Australia and New Zealand for MCC (and he hit 130 against his homeland at Wellington). Lowry was a man who knew his own mind; he decided to leave England, only to come back as captain of the New Zealand touring side in 1927 (1,503 runs and four fine centuries). He was the automatic choice to lead his country in the first official series of Tests against England in 1929–30 and he was back here again, renewing Taunton friendships, as tour skipper in 1931.

Record: 1,820 runs (av 24.27)

WALLY LUCKES (1924–49) was Somerset's second most successful wicket keeper. His strength was his unwavering efficiency and it's hard to remember a dropped catch. The stumpings off Jack White were a model of unshowy brilliance and he was a consistent ally of Wellard and Andrews. His style was admired by other professionals, the ultimate accolade. In 1946 he had eight dismissals in a match at Worcester, was the leading stumper in the country and had a calf-bound book to commemorate the fact presented to him by R. J. O. Meyer. If Somerset's bowling was temporarily loose, Luckes at least never flagged. When Surrey scored 512 at the Oval in 1936 and Glamorgan 574–4 at Newport three years later, he didn't concede a single bye.

After illness in 1930 he was advised to drop down the batting order and take things a little easier for the rest of his cricket career. He still scored 90 not out when going in No 10 in a famous match against Leicester at Bath in 1938; the summer before he'd hit his only county century. Modestly he suggests

Kent's Leslie Ames considerately made it possible by bringing on Frank Woolley for the last few balls.
Record: 5,708 runs (av. 16.21) 827 dismissals (586 caught, 241 stumpings)

J. C. W. MACBRYAN (1911–31) was on the fringe of the Somerset élite, a genuine stylist at the wicket, with the strokes and the polish to go with it. He played once for England, against the South Africans in a 1924 match largely ruined by rain. The competition was intense in those days but he was still considered talented enough to open the innings. He was a good-looking bat but also a fighter and some of his best knocks were on difficult wickets. Jack MacBryan's cut was always worth going to see—and so were the hook and on-drive. He was born at Box, Wiltshire in 1892 and educated at Cheltenham. His Blue at Cambridge didn't come easily. In just over 150 matches for Somerset, his small, dapper appearance in the Cambridge cap was usually a sign that runs were around. He was a prisoner-of-war in 1914–18 and a wound affected his throwing arm. Old-timers who warm winter evenings with memories of highlights from the past invariably cite a MacBryan innings at some time.
Record: 8,372 runs (av 31.01)

BILLY MIDWINTER (1877–82) is inevitably part of Gloucestershire folk-lore. He was almost certainly the only player—in any country—to have been kidnapped. The coup was the devious work of W. G. Grace who arrived with his entourage at Lord's and made off with the padded and apparently gullible member of the Australian touring side. The dubious logic of The Champion was that Midwinter had actually been born in Gloucestershire and he should be playing for his native county. In truth, the player had emigrated with his parents from the Forest of Dean. Australia nurtured him as a cricketer. His playing career is every bit as extraordinary as his Lord's 'capture'; he played eight times for Australia against England—and four for England against Australia. Grace had once been bowled during a tour by Midwinter's round-arm spinner. From that moment the surreptitious plans were laid. The stay with

Gloucestershire was from 1877–82, at £8 a match. Eight years later, back in Australia, he was dead.
Record: 1,603 runs (av 20.04) 232 wickets (15.82)

PERCY MILLS (1902–29) was a popular professional with Gloucestershire from just after the turn of the century. He was a genuine stock bowler, no more than honest medium pace but able to peg away with encouragingly few errors in length and line. Often he shared the attack with Charlie Parker and the two, in their different ways, were capable of bowling right through the innings. It must have been galling to him to have relatively little reward for an afternoon's unrelenting toil in the Bristol sun. Whereas Charlie made his feelings unambiguously clear, Percy never uttered a word of reproach at a dropped catch off his bowling. One of his best seasons was 1926 when he topped 100 wickets. In every sense he was a personable professional with a great affection for the county. As a batsman he once surprised himself by scoring 95.
Record: 823 wickets (av 25.20) 5,052 runs (11.74)

CLIFF MONKS (1935–52) had just over 100 innings for Gloucestershire and bowled fewer than 500 overs. Everyone—not just those who were present—remembers him for one magnificent catch. It's already part of West Country sporting folklore. Middlesex were the visitors to Cheltenham in 1947 and the championship title was at stake. The College ground was packed and the crowd were stunned by Gloucestershire's final defeat by 68 runs. But the Monks catch lives on, even today. R. W. V. Robins, in dazzling form, hit the ball high towards the ropes—and the fair haired stonemason from South Gloucestershire sprinted around the boundary and stretched out a bronzed arm for an incredible catch that prevented a six. His county chances were limited but he was a competent all-rounder and once hit a century against Cambridge in Bristol (1948). He was an intriguingly paradoxical man, strong-minded and gentle, a competitive opponent and a creative village organist and choirmaster.
Record: 1,589 runs (av 18.91) 36 wickets (45.25)

JOHN MORTIMORE (1950–75) was for three years captain of Gloucestershire. He did the job in a way which reflected his personality: efficiently and quietly. His wasn't the expansive personality to dominate a match or fire schoolboys' imaginations. But he had plenty of valued qualities, including a sharp cricketer's brain and a dry sense of humour. When Somerset's Tom Cartwright once let the ball slip from his hands, it trickled to a halt halfway down the wicket. Mortimore, a stickler for convention, made a polite little query to the umpire before scampering to the ball and driving it in golf-style to the boundary.

Test recognition first came to him unexpectedly in November 1958 when Freddie Brown decided he wanted the promising off-spinner to supplement the England team in Australia. 'Morty' got over the shock, flew out without any practice for weeks and excelled as a batsman rather than slow bowler in the final Melbourne Test. He went on to play for his country nine times. His first match for Gloucestershire came in 1950 as a last-minute replacement against the West Indians (such surprises became for him an occupational delight). As a batsman he hit the ball hard and was one of the few to score 10,000 runs and take 1,000 wickets for his county.

Record: 14,917 runs (av 18.34) 1,696 wickets (22.69)

BILLY NEALE (1923–48) was one of the best players of spin in the years between the wars. While some cricketers of greater reputation were apt to betray apprehension as the ball turned capriciously, this Berkeley farmer visibly revelled in the challenge. He played for Gloucestershire from 1923 to 1948, retiring in the same year as Charlie Barnett. His runs, nearly 15,000 of them, were scored with the loving care of a craftsman. He had an unassuming attitude towards his gentle leg-spinners and seldom advanced his claims to be brought on. That was perhaps the county's loss: when there was a wicket to his liking and he could offset lack of practice with an adequate length, he could do bewildering things with the ball. Somerset players of the late 30's will painfully remember one 6–9 spell, as impish as it

112

was unexpected. With those strong country hands of his, he was a fine fielder in the deep.

Record: 14,752 runs (av 23.75) 100 wickets (av 39.70)

GEORGE NICHOLS (1891–99) was born at Fishponds in Bristol so should by rights have played for Gloucestershire. And so he did until he 'changed ends' and became, like Tyler, a willing workhorse who pushed the ball through until Sammy Woods was ready to come back again. The county had few reliable bowlers and the Tyler-Nichols firm was badly in need of a trade union prepared to fight for a more lenient work-load. Apart from being an honest all-round sportsman he had a natural flair for dramatics on and off the field.

He went down to Glastonbury and hit 311 out of 656 on one extraordinary April day. That proved he could bat; then he went along to Norton Fitzwarren, Herbie Hewett's village club, and took all ten wickets for six runs. Cricket was theatre to him —and after he'd finished playing he sat down and wrote a melodrama which was produced on the London stage.

Record: 299 wickets (av 23.42) 2,835 runs (13.82)

RON NICHOLLS (1951–75) maybe had one serious fault. He was too self-effacing. With added self-confidence and a slightly more positive approach at the crease, he would have been an even better opening bat. Not that nearly 24,000 runs and 18 centuries is a modest accomplishment. He made his county debut as a 17-year-old and gradually displayed the application and powers of concentration to make him an ideal opener. Rather too seldom he gave us glimpses of the array of attacking shots he could make; there were times when he visibly pondered the complexities of batting and apprehensively kept his latent brilliance out of sight. At all times he was a quiet and friendly companion, more ready to extol others' sporting merits.

We had to remind him of his 217 at Oxford in the match that produced the record opening stand with Young and the century off the West Indians in 1966. There was also his agile work in the covers and his intermittent, somewhat costly, appearances as an off-spinner. In the winter he dived deftly: a goalkeeper nimble

113

enough to play for Bristol Rovers, Cardiff and Bristol City.
Record: 23,607 runs (av 26.17)

GRAHAME PARKER (1932–51) did an emotional full circle
at the age of 56, bravely turning from teaching—he was house
master at Blundells—back to Gloucestershire cricket. He was
appointed secretary and before long the county's first manager,
at least in the modern sense. From Gloucester's Crypt School,
he went on to excel at both cricket and rugby for Cambridge.
As a rugby full back who played for his county and England he
had the considerable pluck and tactical kicking skill that
becomes a Gloucester man. His cricket was that of a lively all-
rounder—he swung the ball at medium pace and scored runs
attractively.

His county debut was in 1932 and he was, despite the trend,
an amateur thoroughly worth his place. Maybe he wondered if
confidence was misplaced as he started the 1933 season with
five ducks; his maiden century came along before the end of the
summer, to reassure him. Before he opted for an academic
career, there were innings to live long in the memory. His 205-
run stand with Charlie Barnett against Notts at Bristol was one;
his splendid 210 against Kent at Dover was another. He had, it
could be said, a sporting style more extrovert than his own
quietly thoughtful and unassuming manner. In retirement now,
he continues his research into Gloucestershire's cricket and is
seen as the county's valuable unofficial historian.
Record: 1,954 runs (av 18.78) 32 wickets (42.68)

FRED ROBERTS (1887–1905) was one of the early professionals who bowled his heart out for Gloucestershire. He was
a left-arm pace man with a genuine hostility and lift. Not that
he was always used sensibly—or from the right end. Whatever
the whims of his formidable captain, Roberts, still took
virtually a thousand wickets and was a great favourite with the
home crowds. He kept a pub in Montpelier, Bristol for some
time: how he earned those cooling pints after a day's cricketing
toil, minimally praised! Once when the 'Old Man' inexplicably
dropped Roberts and Bill Murch, both committeemen and the

professionals' fan club wanted to know why. 'It wasn't much of a wicket so I thought the bad bowlers were just as likely to get the opposition out as the decent ones. Besides Roberts and Murch were getting a bit uppish.' An unsubstantiated view, cussedly prompted by the 400 or more first innings runs scored off the deputy bowlers.

Record: 967 wickets (av 21.95)

ERNEST ROBSON (1895–1923) is still remembered for the way he won the match against Middlesex at Weston-super-Mare in 1922, with a six in the final over. It's a Somerset memory lovingly passed down from father to son. 'Robbie' represented the best of honest 'professional' toil on the cricket field. He was still bowling unchanged through the innings with Jack White (who else) when he was 49; his last of five centuries for the county came against Worcestershire when he was past 50. Take out the war years and it was still a long and loyal career for Somerset after leaving his native Yorkshire. His batting and bowling were certainly not always memorable on the same day; some of his best scoring came as early as 1902 and his persevering medium-paced bowling brought him hat-tricks against Hampshire in 1898 and Yorkshire (as prized as Lawrence's nearly half a century later) in 1902. That winning six at Weston earned Ernie £50 from an anonymous supporter and it was wholly deserved. He planned to join Braund as an umpire but died before his first appointment.

Record: 12,439 runs (av 17.66) 1,122 wickets (av 26.60)

BRIAN ROSE (1969–) was maybe a surprise choice as captain after Brain Close. In fact, the invitation to him was a wise one and within 18 months he was being widely mentioned as a candidate to lead England, too. He leads the county by example—he's a canny left-hand bat at the top of the order who can reveal forcing shots or go into recession according to the side's needs. The strokes are mostly clean and unflurried. I was there to see his memorable 205 against Northants at Weston-super-Mare and enjoyed the emergent daring late in the innings. He was almost first to the sponsor's tent afterwards for the pint he had so thoroughly earned.

Rose left Kent when still in the carry-cot, was educated at Weston Grammar School and after a county debut in 1969 sensibly qualified as a teacher before returning to county cricket. He impressed Alec Bedser when he came to Taunton to watch Botham and won a place—and three Test appearances— on the 1977–78 tour of Pakistan and New Zealand. He's a thoughtful tactician; and a quiet, likeable and sensitive person. The taunts that followed a collective decision to stretch (not break) the rules for a Benson and Hedges match at Worcester hurt him deeply.

FRED RUMSEY (1963–68) could be a magnificent left-arm pace bowler. When his arm and tail were up, batsmen visibly quaked at the hostility. England sensed his value and chose him five times. He and Ken Palmer gave Somerset a splendidly speedy opening attack; both topped 100 wickets, for instance, in 1963 when they were at their best. Latterly the arm didn't go up quite so high and the frame seemed to broaden but he was still a valuable bowler to have around. He was born at Stepney and had a mildly nomadic cricketing life that started with Worcestershire and ended with Derbyshire where he went, after leaving Taunton, for public relations and fund-raising work. Rumsey had strong views on contractual terms and players' conditions and was one of the men behind the formation of the Cricketers' Association. His wicket tally for Somerset was impressive by any standards.
Record: 520 wickets (av 19.78)

COLIN SCOTT (1938–54), fresh from Downend—Grace territory, after all—made an impressive arrival on the county scene. In only his second season he was picking up 121 wickets (av 22.69) and was looking like a potential new ball specialist for years to come. He was generally thought to be on the short-list for an Australian tour and his old friends from Bristol club cricket believed Gloucestershire had found a winner. His appearance was striking: tall, fair haired and good looking. But the war really put an abrupt end to his cricket aspirations. Like so many other skilful county players he tried to start again afterwards and it was never quite the same. Wickets were more grudgingly given. The youthful zest had receded a little and he was a competent rather than menacing opening bowler. He still took 101 wickets in 1952 and also busied himself snapping up catches at short leg off Tom Goddard's bowling. As a batsman he got to within 10 of the century he often looked capable of reaching from the late middle-order.

Record: 3,375 runs (av 11.92) 531 wickets (31.57)

JIM SEABROOK (1919–35) captained Cambridge in 1928 and hit five centuries for Gloucestershire. He was a left-hander with a neat, attractive style and it was a pity he was not available more often for the county. In the mid-Twenties he was making as few as 12 appearances a season and still scoring nearly 600 runs including a merry and memorable 132 against Essex at Leyton. Much of his best batting was reserved for away matches. In 1928 he went off to Pontypridd and gave the sort of innings of which Haileybury would have been proud. That chanceless 136 was probably his best; but there were a number of match-winning and match-swaying knocks. He didn't seem to need much practice. In 1933 he returned for the Cheltenham Festival match with Leicestershire, his first county match for more than two years, and lustily swung five sixes in a typically appealing century. With more matches, there'd have certainly been more hundreds. 'FJ' took over as acting captain when Bev Lyon was driven off, reluctantly, by business commitments.

Record: 3,371 runs (av 22.47)

C. O. H. SEWELL (1895–1919) was captain and secretary of Gloucestershire from 1913–15, having taken over from Gilbert Jessop. He had the appearance of being slightly supercilious but his bat was companionable enough. At the top of the order, he made his runs sensibly and with ample style. Twice he carried his bat through the innings: a fighting 88 against Yorkshire at Sheffield in 1898 and 114 against Sussex at Bristol seven years later. There were eight centuries, half of them at Bristol; his best, full of polished strokes on a placid Oval wicket, was an innings of 165 immdiately before the First World War. That was quite a notable season for him; he took the train to Taunton and scored a handsome 113 off the neighbouring county. He came in the tradition of old-style amateurs and a few of the discreetly cynical pros never quite knew what to make of him. Most of them, however, admired his batsmanship.

Record: 6,850 runs (av 22.75)

DAVID SHEPHERD (1965–79) always looked rather like a village cricketer: happy face, arms made for sixes and generous waistline. It was hard to imagine him as an eel-like scrum half, which his friends back in North Devon said he once was; also hard to picture him scampering for breathless singles, which in fact he did with zest and unfaltering judgment. He came late (24) to county cricket and signalled his arrival with a confidently belted century in his first match, against Oxford. The county game, with its demanding techniques, never came quite as easily after that and the self-critical Shepherd once or twice pondered whether he should stay. It was to Gloucestershire's benefit that he did.

There were a dozen centuries in all, three of them against Somerset who delayed inviting him to join them while their neighbours, on Reg Sinfield's recommendation, wasted no time. He showed fine form for Devon for five years before that. The blows from his bat had meat and muscle but the strokes could be discriminate and often handsome. He had some of the superstitions of the Devonian and caused great amusement with his antics at the crease whenever the total was 111.

Record: 10,672 runs (av 24.47)

DAVID SMITH (1956–71) was said by some, watching his leisurely run-up to the wicket, to be too slow for the new ball. Neither his team-mates nor opposing batsmen would agree. He didn't believe in wasting energy before releasing the ball. When it did leave his surprisingly strong arms, it dug its way viciously into the turf and hurtled off again at a startling pace. He played five times for his country, in India; then injury put paid to his hopes of more matches in Pakistan. Once he was summoned to join the Test party against the Australians but it didn't result in an appearance. If he was disappointed, he hid it in a philosophical shrug. Above all, he was a wholehearted team man for Gloucestershire, bowling just as long as he was asked. The county in fact asked him a good deal and five times, from 1957–65, he took 100 wickets in a season; his best summer was 1960 (136 wickets—av 20.90). That kind of form earned him a tour to New Zealand. With less emphasis on cricket, he'd have been an even better footballer. As it was he played on the wing for England Boys and had league experience with Bristol City and Millwall.

Record: 1,159 wickets (av 23.68)

HARRY SMITH (1912–35) was perhaps the most efficient of Gloucestershire's distinguished line of wicket keepers. His style was not ostentatious and his shouts not irritatingly excessive. He became Gloucestershire's stumper after the First War and then gave way in 1936 to Andy Wilson, one of his great admirers. In the 1919 season Harry scored a century in each innings off Hampshire at Southampton, demonstrating that he could bat as well as nimbly crouch and cope with the spinners. He played in a single Test, against the West Indians, but if you want to know how unerringly diligent he was, ponder on the Surrey total of 557 for 7 at the Oval in 1927. There were no byes. He was a modest and likeable man, talented enough at soccer to play for Bristol Rovers and Bolton Wanderers. Fellow cricketers will remember him for his prodigious concentration.

Record: 13,330 runs (av 22.59) 706 victims (443 catches, 263 stumpings)

EDWIN 'TED' JAMES TYLER (1891–1907) was the definitive uncomplaining pro. He was a slow left-arm bowler of great merit who opened the attack in Somerset's first match at the Oval and bowled 80 overs before he staggered away from the ground. He was a six-footer with a Kidderminster accent and a much-rewarded tendency to vary the pace of his deliveries, which were flighted rather than spun. Before he qualified for Somerset in 1885 he had a few games for Worcester-

119

shire, for whom he batted pleasantly, as well as taking wickets.

While settling in the West Country he had a few games for Taunton and in a fixture against deadly rivals Bridgwater he scored 59 out of 70 (there were also 8 extras). He had little chance—or perhaps inclination—to bat for Somerset after regularly bowling unchanged. In 1895 he took all 10 wickets for 49 against Surrey at Taunton; three years earlier he had taken 9–33 against Notts on the same ground. Tyler was a popular player who did some coaching at Taunton School. He's said to have first spotted the promise of a schoolboy called . . . J. C. White.

Record: 869 wickets (av 22.26)

ROY VIRGIN (1957–72) was born not far from the county ground in Taunton and it seemed rather sad when he eventually moved on to Northamptonshire. He was a chunky, impressive opening batsman who had a marvellous 1970 season when he scored 2,223 runs for Somerset and seemed on the verge of Test recognition. His 22 centuries for the county were normally a mixture of sturdy watchfulness and emergent cover drives, attractively struck. He was one of a number of local boys of genuine and stylish talent to develop about the same time as if in answer to the hoary taunts of Taunton's 'League of Nations' cricket. Virgin had safe hands, specialised close to the wicket and took 42 catches in the 1966 season.

Record: 15,458 runs (av 28.50)

BRIAN 'BOMBER' WELLS (1951–59) probably had more stories told about him than he scored runs. Here was county cricket's principal jester of the Fifties. His sterling deeds, often with bat from the bottom of the order, are still keeping sports dinners going. There were periods in the long history of Gloucestershire cricket when it was all a rather dour business. 'Bomber' redressed the balance, tossing up his off spinners accompanied by aposite running commentary, or demonstrating with singular good humour how not to judge a short single. He was, in fact, a talented bowler, unlucky enough to be around at the same time as Allen and Mortimore.

Twice, in 1955 and 1956, he took well over 100 wickets. His run-up was a prodigious two paces, frequently reduced to one— to the consternation of batsmen who were still getting comfortable. He was a compositor by trade and printer's ink had its romantic appeal to him; indeed he's been known to write as amusingly as he chats about a game which was to him always something more than an afternoon on a 'slow turner'.
Record: 544 wickets (av 21.18)

PETER WIGHT (1953–65) came over from British Guiana to play some League cricket for Burnley and it seemed inevitable that he would gravitate to the county game. Somerset had the opportunism and vision to offer him a contract, dramatically justified with a century off the Australians in his first match. He tells of the acute disappointment of being quickly caught in the slips in the first innings. Over beer and skittles in a country pub, Richie Benaud consoled him and said Wight would get a hundred before the match was over. The Aussie probably wished he had been less prophetic.

Wight was a stylish stroke-maker, even if he was supposedly none too partial to Trueman at his most belligerent. The slim, graceful batsman scored 222 not out against Kent at Taunton in 1959; his next season was his best, full of attractive runs (2,316), many of them off the front foot. There were 27 centuries and occasional off-break dexterity, as on the day he persuaded Stephenson to let him bowl at Chesterfield in 1957 and finished with 6-24.
Record: 16,965 runs (av 32.75)

ANDY WILSON (1936–55) once used to bowl cunning left-arm slows in the Lord's net until it was suggested he would be a better wicket-keeper. He headed West in a snowstorm in 1936 and became one of Gloucestershire's best. Small, tidy and utterly without flashy tricks, he 'kept' brilliantly to spinners like Goddard—and that surely was the acid test for any stumper. His batting was a valuable bonus. He captained the Young Professionals on the strength of his scoring range, learned from watching Patsy Hendren, also small, the importance of the hook and in 1938 went into the record books for his 239-run eighth wicket stand with Hammond ('He told me to run when he called me and I didn't get a ball for six overs').

There were seven centuries for Gloucestershire including one of 130 when going in No 9, pre-war, at Lord's. He was sound enough to open the innings later, and sharp enough behind the stumps to take 10 catches in a 1953 match against Hampshire at Portsmouth. Wilson started in accountancy and later turned to journalism. His ancestors came from Gloucestershire and he was always happy among farming folk. His helpful, modest manner won him friends at the cattle market and press box—as well, of course, as the county ground.

Record: 10,532 runs (av 25.50) 584 dismissals (416 catches, 168 stumpings)

WILLIAM WOOF (1878–1902) represented the age when the professional didn't only bowl his heart out and chase all round the boundary for more privileged members of the team; he also looked after the baggage and ran the errands. Bill—or 'Woofie' as they always called him at his native Gloucester—was only the second full time pro of the county. He was a slow left-arm spinner, tossing the ball up just as long as Mr Grace decreed. Born in 1859, he first played for Gloucestershire before he was 20 and as such was No 1 in a long and distinguished line of bowlers of his type. The Champion had a high regard for Woof, even if the willing spinner was not always used most advantageously. Maybe a trifle cynical about his Gloucestershire duties on and off the field, Woof became coach at Cheltenham College and was available less frequently for the county. But he was popularly brought back at Cheltenham against the Australians in his final 1902 season. For some years he ran a sports shop in the town.

Record: 602 wickets (av 18.80)

MARTIN YOUNG (1949–64) was supposedly vulnerable against the short-pitched balls. Admittedly the Bristol wicket is slow but he could be a beautiful hooker at Ashley Down, and square-leg never stood a chance. He was possessed of a suave manner and a batting style to go with it. There was nothing stodgy or inelegant about him. Born in Leicestershire, he sampled county cricket at Worcester before arriving at Bristol in 1949. His impact in the years that followed was considerable and Test selectors, grudgingly unsentimental, might logically have given him recognition at least once. He scored 40 centuries for Gloucestershire, 15 of them at Bristol and predictably figured in the record opening stand of 395 against Oxford in 1962. His share was 198. Young's 127 off the formidable West Indies attack at Bristol in 1963 possibly gave him most pleasure. With all that running between the wickets, he was still the county's best outfield.

Record: 23,400 runs (av 31.53)